HILDE ON THE RECORD

MEMOIR OF A KID CRIME REPORTER

Hilde Lysiak

CHICAGO
REVIEW
PRESS

Copyright © 2022 by Hilde Kate Lysiak
All rights reserved
First hardcover edition published in 2022
First paperback edition published in 2023
Published by Chicago Review Press Incorporated
814 North Franklin Street
Chicago, Illinois 60610
ISBN 978-1-64160-903-6

The Library of Congress has cataloged the hardcover edition as follows:
Names: Lysiak, Hilde, 2006– author.
Title: Hilde on the record: memoir of a kid crime reporter / Hilde Lysiak.
Description: Chicago: Chicago Review Press, 2022. | Audience: Ages 8–12 |
    Summary: "Young crime reporter Hilde Lysiak shares, for the first time,
    how she started her own newspaper, the Orange Street News, and how she
    was able to not only survive the ups and downs of her youth but emerge
    from it all with a renewed sense of purpose and confidence"—Provided
    by publisher.
Identifiers: LCCN 2021052943 (print) | LCCN 2021052944 (ebook) | ISBN
    9781641605816 (cloth) | ISBN 9781641605823 (adobe pdf) | ISBN
    9781641605847 (epub) | ISBN 9781641605830 (kindle edition)
Subjects: LCSH: Lysiak, Hilde, 2006– —Juvenile literature. |
    Journalists—United States—Biography—Juvenile literature. | BISAC:
    JUVENILE NONFICTION / Biography & Autobiography / General | LCGFT:
    Autobiographies.
Classification: LCC PN4874.L975 A3 2022 (print) | LCC PN4874.L975 (ebook)
    | DDC 070.92 [B]—dc23/eng/20211122
LC record available at https://lccn.loc.gov/2021052943
LC ebook record available at https://lccn.loc.gov/2021052944

All images are from the author's collection

Cover design and illustration: Natalya Balnova
Typesetting: Nord Compo

Printed in the United States of America

For my mom, Bridget Reddan Lysiak

CONTENTS

PREFACE

WHEN YOU ARE A LITTLE KID, truth is simple. You may not always speak it, but you know it. I'm fourteen now and it feels more complicated. Take memories, for example. When I think back about starting my newspaper, there are the things that I remember, but then there are the stories I have been told. In my case, these stories have not only been passed on by my family and friends; they have also been told by hundreds and thousands of newspapers, magazines, and television shows. Everyone's version of what happened is slightly different from the next.

I spent much of my first six years following my dad around New York City as he reported for the *New York Daily News*. The earliest lesson he taught me was that reporters should never put themselves in the story. That can be avoided by interviewing as many people as possible and asking them the five basic questions: *who, what, where, when*, and *why*. The goal is always to present the reader with enough information to know the truth.

But what happens when the people being interviewed have different descriptions of the same event? *Perspective* refers to the way things are seen from a particular point of view. Two people could

Hilde, twelve, searching for leads on her bike.

witness the same event yet report two different stories. This is not necessarily because either person is lying but rather because they have different perspectives of the event. Take a car accident, for example. A person standing on the right side of the street, slightly behind a tree, may report events much differently from the person watching from the other side of the street without a tree in their way. Even when a reporter does a fantastic job of presenting many people's stories, in the end, the reader is left to decide what they think happened.

I find myself in a strange position in writing this book. This is the first time I will be putting myself in the story, although it won't be the first time I have been written about. When, at age nine, I found myself going viral for being the first to report on a homicide in my town, I was confronted head-on by the challenge of people's perspectives. Here is a list of ways my reporting was described in the following days:

- Precocious
- Sensationalist trash

- Heroic
- Complete joke
- Indecent
- Disrespectful
- Brave
- Innovative
- Refreshing
- Embarrassing

In addition to these adjectives, I was praised for empowering girls but also told that I should be home playing with dolls and having tea parties. So yeah, perspective. Millions of people read or watched my news coverage with almost as many different reactions.

This book is my attempt to tell the story from my perspective. In the end, what you think is up to you.

1

THE BEGINNING

S NUGGLY, CALM, JOYFUL, *affectionate, peaceful, imaginative, nature loving.* These are words my parents use to describe me as a young child. My memories of this time are just three-dimensional versions of the photographs in frames around our house. I remember my early childhood in almost the exact way my family retells it, just with more color and movement.

For the first five years or so, I wore little more than my waist-long hair and multicolored rain boots. I had a thing with texture. I only liked fabric that felt smooth and flat. I could only touch one side of the special blanket my older sister gave me as a baby, and even though the right pair of leggings felt OK against my skin, I preferred not to wear clothes. I have always had a lot of hair, and by the time I was two, it hung all the way down my back. Even though I was born in the big city, I always felt best when I was able to run barefoot in the grass and dig in the dirt. This all earned me the joking reputation of "flower child," "free spirit," or "hippie." It is funny all these years later to compare those words to the ones the media would eventually use to describe me—words like "precocious," "spitfire," "rebel," or even "bada**." Although they never quite felt like me, it is interesting to think about how I went from laid-back nature girl to crime-solving sleuth.

I was born in Brooklyn, New York, on November 2, 2006. I lived with my mom, dad, and three-year-old sister, Izzy. We were a happy foursome but quite different from one another. Izzy was my polar opposite. She was loud and bold and actually cried hysterically the first time her bare feet touched grass. Not only did she refuse to play dolls with me, she disliked most toys. While I would disappear for hours creating new worlds with my toys, Izzy would practice for the day she would become a famous singer. She would occasionally play with me as long as she could be the teacher and I, her student. She was bossy. I don't think she'd mind me saying, she still is. But it worked for us because I was usually happy to be the student. This has served me well in life.

My mom was the creative type. She loved books and poems and movies and music. She read to us often and played her songs loudly so that we could dance. She was less concerned with how many words we could read and more focused on the stories we could tell. Even though she was trained to be a high school English teacher, she and my dad made the decision that she would stay home with us instead of working. This would become especially important as my dad's career took off.

My dad was a reporter for the fifth-biggest newspaper in the country—the *New York Daily News*. Crime doesn't keep a schedule. Natural disasters don't necessarily happen between nine and five. This meant my dad's work routine was never predictable. While most of my friends' parents left for work after breakfast and came home for dinner, my dad might be home for hours in the daytime but then called away at a moment's notice, sometimes for a week or two, to report on something that could be all the way on the other side of the country.

One summer when I was little, my parents wanted to get us out of the city for a while. My dad had been traveling a lot for work, and our family desperately needed time together. We rented a beautiful cabin on a lake in Maine for three weeks. The first ten days or so were amazing. We swam every day, hiked and explored, played endless rounds of gin rummy, and sat around the fire each night, usually with my dad telling the ghost stories Izzy and I loved best.

But 1,600 miles away, a hurricane was brewing. On the seventh anniversary of the devastating Hurricane Katrina, Hurricane Isaac threatened to bring destruction again to the city of New Orleans. Isaac did not care that without my dad, no one would tell ghost stories (my mom hates scary stuff). His bosses at the *New York Daily News* did not think about how much Izzy and I needed to spend the rest of our vacation with him or how my mom hated to drive long distances by herself. There was a huge national story about to break, and my dad was the best reporter they had. So, ten days into our lovely little lake vacation, we drove the hour to the Portland airport and watched as my dad went off to cover a hurricane.

Watching my dad go made me feel split in two. On the one hand, I was very sad to see him leave. It felt like we needed more family time. That had been the whole purpose of the trip, yet he left. Again. Looking back now, I think my dad was also really sad to leave. I think he may have felt guilty too. On that particular trip, I remember him giving my mom a bunch of money to take us to the big mall in Portland after we dropped him at the airport. I have to admit, it was a good distraction at first. We went to Build-A-Bear (a place my mom usually avoided like the plague) and got to make any stuffed animal we wanted, complete with all the accessories. My favorite part was the heart they sewed in at the end. Afterward, we ate a big meal where my mom, who usually only let us drink water, ordered us lemonades.

On the drive back to the cabin, listening to the sound of my new bear's heartbeat, I couldn't help but think about what my dad was doing. There was a part of me that was worried about his safety, but the biggest part felt excitement. My dad was an adventurer! A kind of superhero. Without much notice or knowledge of the situation, my dad would fly into areas and have to figure out what was going on. He was like the eyes and ears for millions of people around the country who needed to know what was happening. Imagine if someone you loved lived thousands of miles away in a city where a hurricane was about to strike. At first, you would be able to talk to them on the phone to know they were safe. But eventually, if the hurricane was bad enough, it might become difficult to communicate with them. You would most likely feel very scared and concerned for their safety. You would have many questions. Were they able to evacuate? Are the dams holding? What kind of emergency help is available in the area? A reporter could be the link that answers those questions and keeps you updated.

Riding in the back of the car to our cabin, I had so many questions. I realized if I could interview anyone in that moment, it would be my dad. I thought about how he did it. I imagined how brave he would have to be to go into those dangerous situations, how calm he would have to stay in order to figure out what was happening. But how?

I also knew that many times, the stories he covered had very sad endings. Even though my dad was almost always smiling and joking, there were times when he came home and was quiet or even cranky. I wondered if it was because he felt sad about some of the things he saw while working. Was he ever scared? Did he ever worry that he wouldn't make it back home to us?

As I snuggled my bear to sleep, I vowed to get those answers as soon as my dad returned home.

2

ANOTHER LANGUAGE

———

"**I CAN'T BELIEVE** I had to leave vacation for that."

"Yeah, but if it was worth leaving for, that would mean a city was destroyed."

"Yeah, you're right. I guess I was looking at it pretty selfishly."

My parents were in the living room having coffee talk on the first morning my dad was back. Hurricane Isaac had spared the city of New Orleans, changing at the last minute to a tropical storm and passing to the west of the city. That was great news for the people of New Orleans, but it was not exactly *great news* for the paper. I was in my playroom a few feet away pretending to build a castle with my blocks so I could listen in.

"Well," my mom said, "I get it. It stinks that you had to go. The girls say they don't care, but I can tell it's on their minds. Hilde didn't let go of that bear the rest of the trip."

"Yeah, I wish I had a few days off to be with them here," Dad said. "At least I just have to cover that parade today. Shouldn't take too long."

Hearing that, I saw my opening.

"Can I go with you?" I asked as I accidentally knocked my blocks over trying to make a graceful entrance into the living room. (Notice "graceful" was not one of the words used to describe me.)

It's not like Izzy and I hadn't gone reporting with my dad before. We had been lucky enough to accompany him on some of his out-of-town trips. When the *New York Daily News* needed him to cover something in a different part of the country, it would pay for his hotel for as long as he needed to be there. There were times when this location was someplace super cool, like the beach or Martha's Vineyard. If my dad thought he might be there for a while, he would ask my mom to bring us. On these trips, we might be exploring the area as a family, but my dad would get a call and need to stop somewhere to interview someone. Izzy and I would always have to stay in the car with our mom, but I would try my hardest to listen to what was happening outside. Later, if the story wasn't too upsetting, my dad would give us some of the details he had uncovered.

It was the same way back in New York. Sometimes, one of our family outings would be detoured because my dad had to report on something. Because of this, my sister and I got to see many different neighborhoods all across New York City. These weren't the tourist areas. These places were where the everyday people lived and worked. Izzy and I have sat for many hours inside little neighborhood restaurants with my mom, passing the time eating the local food while my dad was off interviewing people. We tried patties in Jamaica, Queens; dim sum in Sunset Park; Hungarian food on the Lower East Side; Russian food in Brighton Beach; and some of the best Italian food on Arthur Avenue in the Bronx. There was even a neighborhood where a little old lady would lower a basket down to the street. You would put your money in, she'd raise the basket, and then lower it again with delicious homemade Italian ice. This, of course, was my favorite.

Reporting was just a way of life for all of us. It's like growing up with a grandmother who speaks another language. It may sound weird to one of your friends who comes over, but to you, it is just normal. And even though no one is trying to teach you to speak that language, you probably know some words just because you've been around it, listening. But I was done just being in the background, listening. I wanted to see my dad in action from start to finish. I didn't want to be around the corner eating Korean chicken wings (so good, by the way!). I wanted to be next to him while he was asking the questions. Plus, it would give me alone time with him to ask all *my* questions.

My parents, a bit startled by the crashing blocks, looked at me and then at each other.

"Oh, Hilds, you can't—" my mom started.

"Sure," my dad interrupted.

The two of them turned to each other, my mom with a confused look on her face.

"Ah—why not—it'll be fun. It'll give us some time to catch up. It's just a parade," my dad said.

Neither one of us was prepared for just how wrong he would be.

3

LIFE'S NO PARADE

RAFFIC WAS LIGHT on this Brooklyn Saturday. I sat in the back of my dad's beat-up Hyundai Elantra as it careened through the city streets. We were headed to the West Indian Day Parade in the neighborhood of Crown Heights. Every year on the first Saturday in September, anywhere between one and three million people crowded the streets to celebrate West Indian heritage.

"This should be super fun, Hilds," my dad said. "But it's going to be really crowded, so you need to stay by my side at all times."

That wouldn't be a problem for me. I couldn't wait to spend the day right next to my dad, watching him in action. As we came closer, my dad rolled the windows down. The sound of steel drums filled the car.

"Calypso," my dad told me. "It started out in Trinidad and Tobago. Today is a day the people from the islands can remember and celebrate their culture. Music and dancing are huge parts of that."

My dad, much to my mom's annoyance, never drove around looking for a good parking spot. He loved to walk almost as much as he hated driving around aimlessly. He would much rather park a mile away than waste his time searching for a spot. On this day, I swear he must have parked two miles away. As we walked, I ignored the tired feeling spreading through my little legs and instead held on tightly to my dad's hand as the sound of steel drums drew closer.

At first the streets were filled with the normal weekend foot traffic. But as the music became louder, it was obvious something special was happening. Men and women dressed in brightly colored clothes crowded the sidewalks. There were so many interesting things, I didn't know where to look. I turned my head to the right just in time to see six women dressed in orange beaded bikinis wearing huge feathers on top of their heads. Many people carried or wore flags from the different West Indian islands. My stomach began to growl as the smell of jerk chicken and meat patties filled the air.

I looked up at my dad and saw a smile spread across his face. I hadn't even seen him interview anyone yet, but I already knew just how incredible his job was. I thought about my friends' parents, most of whom spent their workday behind a desk in an office. I couldn't imagine what it would be like to not go outside all day long. I knew right then and there that whatever I did, I needed to have the feeling of freedom I felt that day walking hand in hand with my dad.

But the joyful mood was about to quickly change. As we moved about with the crowd, my dad's hand slipped from mine. His pace slowed just a bit. I looked up to see him taking a phone call. Within what seemed like only seconds, Dad had grabbed my hand again and was swiftly pulling me in the opposite direction of everyone else. The relaxed smile I had seen on his face only moments before was replaced with a tight line across his lips. My voice, calling up, "What's going on?" was lost among the steel drums.

The crowd thinned as we moved toward our parked car. I tried as hard as I could to keep up with my dad's pace, but he was moving so quickly and I had already walked so much. Sensing this, my dad bent down and picked me up. In his arms, I knew he would be able to hear me. But when I began to ask again what was going on, I was interrupted by the sound of his phone ringing.

"So, it was a stray bullet? How old again? Good Lord. All right, yeah, I can be there in thirty minutes."

4

CHANGE OF PLANS

MY DAD HUNG UP THE PHONE and put me down.

"I know you're tired, kiddo, but you're going to have to walk now. There's been a change of plans and I need to figure out where I'm going. We can talk in the car, but for right now, I need to focus. OK?"

It didn't really feel OK, but I also didn't want to complain. It seemed like something more important than me was happening. I know that probably sounds sad, but I don't think it's the worst thing to realize as a kid that you are not the center of the universe. I thought about how my mom was always telling us to "practice our patience." This seemed about as good a time as any.

Back in the car, as I watched my dad tap around on his GPS, I realized we weren't going home. My patience felt like a giant balloon about to burst. Just when it felt like I couldn't stand it anymore, my dad started to talk.

"OK, Hilds," he began. "Something bad has happened." Seeing the look of horror on my face, he quickly added, "Not to anyone we know.

"But I don't have time to take you home. If I drove back to Bay Ridge right now, by the time I got all the way up to the Bronx, the *Post* would already be there."

The *New York Post* was like an annoying relative you never wanted to see who always seemed to show up anyway. The rival newspaper to the *New York Daily News*, it was always sending its best reporters to compete against my dad. It's kind of like a game of tic-tac-toe—the first person to go has a huge advantage. The first reporter on the scene may see details or be able to interview witnesses that might be gone only moments later. Bay Ridge was twenty minutes in the opposite direction of the Bronx. And I knew from our family outings that, depending on traffic, it could sometimes take an hour to drive all the way up there from Brooklyn. If my dad drove me home, that meant he might not make it on the scene for close to an hour and a half. By then, the *Post* would probably have something up online. My dad just couldn't risk it.

Although my dad looked stressed, I couldn't have been happier. It felt like our day together had just started, and I didn't want it to end. We drove for what felt like an eternity before my dad started talking.

"So not everyone is able to live in a neighborhood that is safe like Bay Ridge," he began. "I guess you probably know that by now," he said, meeting my eyes in the rearview mirror.

I nodded my head, not saying a word. I knew he could get another phone call at any minute, and I didn't want to wait any longer for what he was about to tell me.

"Well, many times these neighborhoods are dangerous because of gangs. These are groups of people who form together almost like a team, but instead of playing games or sports, they commit crimes together. A lot of them sell drugs. Sometimes different gangs fight each other over which gang has rights to sell drugs on what street or corner. Now, there are many good people who live in these neighborhoods, but, unfortunately, even though they don't commit crimes, they are often in danger because of the people who do."

I thought about what my dad was saying. Izzy and I had been in many neighborhoods that didn't look as nice as Bay Ridge, but we never felt unsafe. I wondered if we had ever been to a place where there were gangs.

"So, what I'm about to say is very sad, Hilds, and I'm honestly not sure I should even be telling you. But here we are, and I hope this isn't one of those moments you're going to be telling your therapist about years from now . . ."

I wished he would just say it before we got interrupted and I had to wait longer. My patience practicing was wearing thin.

"So, a four-year-old boy was playing in the playground in front of his apartment building, and a car, probably full of gang members, pulled up and began shooting. They weren't trying to hit the boy . . . they were most likely trying to hit a rival gang member that was behind where the boy was playing, but, well—they missed and . . . the boy died."

I'd be lying if I said I wasn't shocked. It's not that I didn't know that bad things happened. This just felt much closer than I had ever been. Immediately, I understood why it was such a big deal for my dad to be bringing me on this story. I needed to act tough so he didn't regret it.

"Did they catch the people who did it?" I asked, thinking it best to stick to the reporting.

"No," he said. "That's why it's so important we get there fast, so we can interview as many witnesses as possible. We might even be interviewing the boy's mother. I've had to do this many times, and it never really gets easier. Losing a child is probably the hardest thing anyone can go through, Hilds. She will obviously be extremely upset."

We arrived in the Bronx neighborhood of Morrisania quickly. Traffic was light on the drive and our talking made the trip feel even faster. The Forest Houses where the boy had lived stretched high into the sky and filled the entire block with giant apartment buildings. These buildings were public housing—apartments that are provided by the government at a lower cost. There were many of them through-out New York City. And almost all of them wrapped around large playgrounds. Izzy and I always talked about how cool it would be to have a playground right outside our door.

My dad steered his car into a spot right in front of the playground. But instead of noticing the swing sets or basketball courts, I immediately caught a glimpse of what looked like hundreds of candles set on the sidewalk. Scattered around them were flowers and teddy bears and a few basketballs. Adults and children huddled together in small groups, many of them crying. As my dad helped me out of the car, one woman moved to the side and I saw that hanging on the fence was a giant picture of a little black boy in a baseball cap. He barely looked older than a baby. My mind raced with a million different thoughts: *He looks so young. Who could do such a thing? How will his family ever feel good again?* My dad gave my hand one final squeeze as he looked me in the eye as if to say, *Be tough—it's going to be OK.*

Over the next two hours, it became apparent that even though there were witnesses around, the police were yet to identify the person who killed the boy. I watched carefully as my dad seemed to balance two different pieces of information that were necessary for the story. The first was painting the picture of who the little boy was. This meant interviewing his closest relatives and friends. The other centered around trying to find video footage of the shooting and then interviewing witnesses to see if a suspect's name could be determined.

After getting out of the car, my dad immediately began talking to the people gathered at the vigil. Most of them were residents of the Forest Houses and knew of the boy and his family but were not close friends or relatives. Within minutes, my dad had the boy's mother's name. I listened as he asked over and over again if anyone knew which apartment she lived in. Finally, after about fifteen minutes, my dad and I were on our way up to her apartment.

Now, one might imagine that the mood between me and my dad was very serious. But—and I'm not sure if this was only for my benefit—as we walked across the courtyard toward the building's entrance, my dad began laughing.

"OK, here's the thing, Hilds," he began with a giggle. "My photographers and I have a little game we play called Elevator or Stairs. You see, many times, the same people who are responsible for the crime in these areas are also the kind of people who don't really have respect for others. Not surprising, right? Well, even though so many of the residents here keep their spaces nice and clean, many times the common areas like the hallways, elevators, and stairs are really dirty and messy. It's like your Mammy used to say: 'One bad apple spoils the bunch.' A small group of disrespectful people living here throw their garbage around the common areas and ruin it for the rest of the residents."

"So, what's the game?" I asked.

"Well, I've seen some super nasty things, Hilds. Not just trash but actual human poop, dirty drug needles, and things you are too young to even know about. That's usually in the stairs. So, you might be thinking, why not just take the elevator? Well, the problem with the elevator is they are very small, maybe not quite as dirty, but you can get stuck in there with some people you'd probably rather not be stuck with."

"Like the people who make the gross messes?" I asked.

"Right. And remember those people are also usually the ones who—"

"—commit the crimes," I interrupted, feeling like I already knew what choice I'd make between stairs and elevator.

"Exactly," said my dad. "When I work these stories with my photographer, we always toss a coin to decide which one we'd take. So, seeing as we haven't met up with our photographer yet, I'll let you make the choice today."

"Stairs," I said without hesitation. I'd take dirty over danger any day.

As we began the climb all the way up to the fifth floor where the boy had lived with his mother, I studied my dad. He seemed so calm and focused. That really impressed me because I was not feeling quite so relaxed. My dad had been right about the stairs. There was garbage lining the steps and it smelled the way Bay Ridge did on a Sunday morning after the bars put the trash out overnight. It was a sour smell, and it was making my tummy feel queasy. I considered if I wanted to go home (not that it was really an option). I thought about what I'd normally be doing on a Saturday afternoon—either playing in my playroom or at the playground with my mom and Izzy. I imagined walking down those stairs, out the door, and across the courtyard to my mom's waiting car.

For a moment a wave of longing came over me. But just as quickly, it was replaced with a feeling of wrongness. Leaving didn't feel right. Leaving would feel like quitting a thousand-piece puzzle that you had been working on for weeks. Something bad had happened. If people didn't know about it, how would things like this ever stop? My dad needed to get the story out so the people who did this could be held responsible. If I could play even the smallest part in that, it was something I was not ready to give up.

It took only two knocks before the boy's mother answered the door. It was the first time I experienced someone in shock. I was expecting crying and screaming, but instead this woman looked like she was not even inside her own body. Her eyes were wide but unfocused. My dad introduced himself and asked if he could have a moment of her time. The woman said yes and sat us around her kitchen table.

For the next twenty minutes or so, the boy's mother showed us pictures and told us about what kind of person he had been. What surprised me most about how my dad interviewed the woman was how little he spoke. He wasn't doing a lot of talking. He was listening. My dad took pictures with his phone of the photos she had so that the *Daily News* would be able to show its readers what the boy looked like.

At one point, when the mother was talking about how much he loved his baby brother, she began crying. And when the crying started, it did not stop. I watched from my seat at the table as my dad gently touched her arm, thanked her for her time, and said how sorry he was about what had happened to her son.

"Just let them know my son is real. He is more than just a name in a bad story. He is, I mean, he was, a good boy . . ." she said.

5

A SMALL SILVER LINING

THE REST OF OUR AFTERNOON consisted of going into convenience stores—or *bodegas*, as they are often called in New York City—that were anywhere close to the Forest Houses. Not every one we went in had surveillance cameras, but my dad was able to find two that did. Sometimes the owners of the bodegas were more willing to show a reporter the video footage than they were the police. The police could force them, but not without first getting a warrant—a document issued by a judge that gives a police officer the right to make searches, seize property, or make arrests. That would take some time.

On this particular day, my dad got lucky—one of the owners who refused to show the video to the police agreed to let my dad see it. Even though my dad's goal was to find the criminals who shot the little boy, if he was successful, it would mean the video footage would also show the little boy getting shot. My dad, not wanting to risk me seeing such a thing, set me up with a drink and a cookie in the front of the store. I remember playing with a little black one-eyed cat as my dad went in the back with the owner to watch the video.

After what seemed like forever, my dad returned to the front of the store. He looked a little paler than before.

"Ready, kiddo? I think we got what we needed. Let's get you home."

On the ride back to Bay Ridge, my dad told me he was able to get a good photo of the man who was in the passenger seat of the car that fired the shots that killed the little boy. What had taken him so long in the back of the store was that he was "filing" his story with his editors. Filing is when you send all the information you get while out reporting so that the news desk can get the story up online. My dad was able to send in the interviews he did with the people at the vigil and the mother, the pictures she gave him of the little boy, and also the surveillance footage of the possible suspect. Another reporter was going to follow up with that picture, asking anyone nearby if they knew who the possible suspect was.

"So, what will the police do now that they have the picture of the person who may have done it?" I asked.

"Well, Hilds, this might seem a little strange, but I didn't give the footage to the police. They will see it once they see my story up online. Reporters don't work for the police. They work for the people. And if I gave it to them first, they would send it out to everyone and then my story wouldn't be exclusive. My editors wouldn't appreciate that very much."

Seeing my confusion, my dad continued, "An exclusive is when you are the only one to have a piece of information. Half a million people will see my story. And now that it's out, the police will have it too, and so will all the other newspapers. So, getting it as an exclusive is just a little silver lining in this otherwise horrible day."

"And helping catch the suspect would be the best silver lining, wouldn't it?" I asked my dad.

"You're so right, kiddo. So right."

6

THE LAST TEACHER
ON THE STAGE

SINCE THAT DAY WITH MY DAD, my parents and I have been asked many times if reporting was an "appropriate" thing for a little girl to be doing. Didn't it make me "afraid, or sad, or traumatized"? Weren't my parents worried it was "robbing me of my childhood"?

The very simple answer is no. The longer explanation involves a mixture of things—balance, I suppose, between reporting and playing and schooling and many hours of discussion about the events I'd witness both while tagging along with my dad and, later, as I'd begin reporting for my own newspaper, the *Orange Street News*.

After the day at the Forest Houses, my dad began bringing me along more often. For the most part, he would take me out on fun stories, like when a group of wild turkeys was terrorizing residents in Staten Island or when the Rockefeller Center Christmas tree was purchased from a farm in Pennsylvania only a few minutes from where my grandparents lived. Occasionally, we would get detoured by a crime story—which I loved—but, for the most part, I was a normal kid who just happened to love reporting and hanging out with her dad. I was incredibly happy.

I've heard my Grammie tell my parents, "It's never the things you worry about that you need to worry about." It was something she would say that meant that people fret over small things when usually the things that are really stressful are things you would never imagine. So while many people were worried about me being exposed to crime reporting, what they never saw coming was that my biggest stress to date would be from a very boring, typical kid activity: kindergarten.

The summer of 2011 brought many changes. On July 25, we welcomed my younger sister, Georgia, to the family. Again, everyone was worried about me—how would I feel now that I was no longer the baby? I overheard both my grandmothers warning my mom that I might, basically, freak out. But I was so excited! Georgie was the silliest baby. She had bright red hair and was really strong. We joked that she was going to have a six-pack because she would raise her head and shoulders off the bed in what looked like a sit-up. She also made crazy-old-man grunting noises that kept us all laughing.

That summer my dad didn't have to travel very much. I remember my mom wearing Georgie in a wrap on her front while we went about our usual activities, like going out to breakfast and to the playground to play in the sprinklers, with my dad walking beside us. Being a family of five gave me a warm, full feeling.

When Georgia was about six weeks old, summer vacation was over and school started back up. Izzy was going into the third grade at the same public school she had been attending since kindergarten. I hadn't really gone to school yet, aside from a few hours a week at the preschool around the corner. Kindergarten would be different. This was all day, five days a week. Even though Izzy seemed to really love school, I had my doubts about it. It seemed like she was gone forever. I couldn't really imagine being away from my toys, my mom, and now my baby sister for that long.

Hilde, four, on the morning of her first day of kindergarten.

Doubts or not, I found myself being herded into the giant auditorium of PS 185 with hundreds of other kindergartners. Some kids were skipping and laughing, a few were crying, and many were clutching their parents' hands with a look of quiet shock on their faces. Even though I felt a little like crying, I took my seat next to my mom without a word or a tear.

The whole mood of the place was a bit like a weird game show. For some reason, the school wouldn't tell the parents who their child's teacher was until the first morning of class. Over the summer, they sent us necklaces we were to wear on the first day. I think mine was in the shape of a school bus and had a number on it. That number was somehow linked to who our teacher was, but we really didn't know any more than that.

As we were all seated in the auditorium for the big reveal, I was a little distracted by the fact that baby Georgie was starting to cry in the carrier on my mom's front. We were in the middle of the row of seats, with no way to get out, and once Georgie got crying, it could be really loud. And embarrassing. Not exactly what I wanted on my first day. Luckily, my mom very casually started nursing her, and all was calm again.

That is, until I looked at the stage. Sitting there like prize ponies were the kindergarten teachers. I can't remember exactly, but there were at least seven or eight of them. They each held a number. These numbers, I would find out, matched the ones on our necklaces. I scanned the stage, taking mental note of each teacher. The first six or seven looked very similar: young and perky with big bubbly grins on their faces. *Not too bad*, I thought. But when my eyes stopped at the last teacher on the stage, a feeling of dread passed through me. There stood a larger, gray-haired woman dressed all in black. She looked older than my grandmothers. But unlike my grandmothers, she wasn't smiling. In fact, she looked kind of angry. My mom, sensing my distress, gave my hand a quick squeeze and a reassuring smile. Years later, we laugh about this moment as she admits feeling exactly the same way about the last teacher on the stage.

I tried to calm myself down. What were the odds that I'd get the angry-looking teacher? As a four-year-old, my math skills might not have been very sharp, but I understood there was only a small chance that she would be my teacher. After a short welcome announcement, the principal began calling groups of children up to meet their teacher. I watched as the crowd began to thin. Parents left down the aisles as their kids joined their class and disappeared through the auditorium doors into the giant school. When there were only two teachers left on the stage, I began to sweat. I started to have a very bad feeling about kindergarten.

I was right, of course. When the last number was called for the final happy-looking teacher, my fate was sealed. The last teacher on the stage would be mine. My mom gave me a tight squeeze and probably said something reassuring that I can't remember. I was too busy trying to make one foot follow the other up toward the stage, even though I felt frozen in place.

Mrs. Green was actually a nice woman. She had six children of her own and many, many grandchildren. She had been teaching school for forty years. She just was what my great-grandmother Mammy would call a "no-nonsense" woman. She was focused on the things that needed to be done and had little room for fun or distraction. Until I started going to Mrs. Green's classroom, my life had been mostly about fun. My mom never pressured us to learn to read or know math facts. She believes that children learn through play. But there was very little play in Mrs. Green's class, and, before long, I found myself feeling stressed out and very unhappy.

My mom remembers more of the details of this time than I do. My most vivid memory is of having to go up to Mrs. Green's desk, where she would take words out of a blue folder that we were expected to read. I remember feeling the bottom of my stomach drop out every time she called my name. I had a hard time remembering the words and could feel her disappointment each time I did not know. Apparently, during this time I also started biting my nails and chewing on the sleeves of my clothes. My parents tell me that I became withdrawn and seemed unhappy.

My mom went in to have a meeting with Mrs. Green to discuss the changes in me. I was not at the meeting, and my parents felt I was too young to hear all of what was discussed that day. Later, my mom would tell me the story of my Thanksgiving turkey. Apparently, Mrs. Green had her own list of words to describe me:

- Unmotivated
- Disorganized
- Immature
- Scattered
- Inattentive

To demonstrate how true this was, Mrs. Green drew my mom's attention to the homemade turkeys around the classroom.

"See these turkeys," she said as my mom's eyes glanced around the room. "*That* one is Hilde's."

When my mom failed to provide the look of shock and horror Mrs. Green clearly was expecting over my construction paper turkey, Mrs. Green pointed out, "Hilde's is the only one without a snood. She had a snood, but she was so disorganized and messy, she lost hers."

My mom said she would have started laughing at the ridiculousness of the situation if it weren't for the fact that this absurdity was where I was spending six hours a day, five days a week.

Mrs. Green did not share my mom's view of education, creativity, play, or success. Mrs. Green talked about "college preparedness" in kindergarten. My mom talked about the power of our imaginations. In our home, we felt free. Our parents made us all feel smart and interesting. If we came up with an idea for a play or an art show, they would help us carry tables outside to set up or perform. In Mrs. Green's class, I felt stupid and stuck. Like I couldn't do anything right. Like *I* wasn't right.

Around this time, my dad got sent to cover a story in Florida near the beach. After a week turned into ten days of being gone, he had a feeling it was going to be a long assignment. Since things weren't really going so well for me in kindergarten, my mom decided we should join him. I'll never forget, after having another bad day in Mrs. Green's class, coming down the stairs at PS 185 into the schoolyard where my mom picked me up. As soon as I saw her face,

I knew something exciting was about to happen—my mom is terrible at hiding a secret.

"Hey, kiddo! I have something for you," she said, handing me a bag from inside her purse.

I reached in and pulled out a brand-new bathing suit. It was freezing cold and cloudy in Brooklyn. I didn't quite understand what this gift was for. I looked at her, confused.

"Let's drive to Florida and see Dad! I think we could all use a little sunshine, don't you?"

It may just be wishful remembering, but I swear my mom looked at Mrs. Green when she said those last words.

We ended up staying in Florida for four weeks. The story my dad was working on involved a teenage boy who was shot and killed by an older man. The older man said he was attacked and was defending himself. Other people said the teenager wasn't doing anything wrong and that he was shot because he was Black. A story like this is another great example of perspective. There was one event but very different opinions of what happened. Because of that, my dad needed to interview many, many people in order to try and get the truth.

One afternoon while we were there, my dad had a few free hours, so we went out exploring as a family. At one point we ended up at one of those old-fashioned photo places where you dress up like characters from the past and get your picture taken. Even though I had been away from Mrs. Green's classroom for a week or two, I still wasn't feeling like myself. It's not like I was really thinking about her blue folder with words I couldn't remember or anything; in fact, I wasn't really thinking about kindergarten at all. Still, the feeling I had in Mrs. Green's class stayed with me. I felt a little nervous inside, like something was always wrong. And I didn't want to be the center of attention (something I usually loved). So when my parents thought it'd be super fun to get us dressed up in costumes to have our pictures taken, I started to feel *really* nervous. I didn't want the people at the photo place looking at me.

I refused to have the picture taken. At first my parents tried to talk me into it, but after a bit they backed off, sensing something wasn't quite right with me. Later, as Izzy and I played with baby Georgie in our vacation room, I overheard my parents talking.

"She's just not herself," my mom said. "I thought she just needed a little break and then we could power through the rest of the school year, hope for better in first grade. I mean, Izzy has always loved it there."

"Hilde is not Izzy, though, is she?" my dad wondered aloud.

"No. And I'm worried this experience is dimming her light," my mom added.

My parents talk a lot about dimming lights. I've asked them about it as I've gotten older, and they say it goes along with their one main parenting belief: *just don't screw them up*. Basically, my parents think kids come into the world with potential that is unique to them. Think of the potential as a little light inside the child. A parent's job is to help guide them in a way that allows that light to shine and protects them from anything that would put out or dim that light. Turns out, kindergarten was the first thing that they would need to protect me from.

"We can't let that happen," my dad said.

"No. I think I'm done, Matt. I'm going to pull her out."

7

THE LONG ONE

I SPENT THE REST OF MY KINDERGARTEN YEAR at home, playing with my toys and going on errands with my mom. She never sat me down and made me try to read words like Mrs. Green did. But she did read many books to me. Soon, I started to recognize enough of the words that I could pull books off our shelves and read them on my own. I spent so much time going grocery shopping that eventually I knew the value of paper money and coins. Sometimes my mom would let me go into the bakery myself and get a croissant. I knew to hand them two dollars and that they would give me forty cents in change, or twenty cents if I could convince my mom to let me have the one with chocolate inside. The nervous feeling began to leave me. Being at home felt right. *I* felt right again.

When first grade came, I went to a private Lutheran school. The classes were small, and we spent a lot of time playing and singing. We had gym class a few days a week, and as long as it wasn't too cold, we went to the playground. I didn't feel nervous there. The teachers and administrators knew how much I loved going reporting with my dad and even let me take a day off here and there to go with him. If I couldn't have done that, I would not have seen my dad much at all that year.

Hilde, five, finds a happy home for first
grade at Leif Ericson Day School in
Brooklyn.

For some reason, 2012 was a very busy news year. There were
even a few times my dad came home from a trip away and was sent
back out the same day to cover a story in a completely different part
of the country. My mom always tried to make my dad's absences fun
for us. We had a routine where we would order Thai takeout and
eat it while watching HGTV—something my dad would never do. I
wasn't a big fan of HGTV, but if you put enough spring rolls in front
of me, I'd watch anything.

We definitely enjoyed this, but we all really missed my dad. One
time, after an especially long trip, my dad came home and went to
scoop up baby Georgie, who was probably around eight months old,
but she began screaming hysterically. She had forgotten who he was.

My dad still talks about this as the moment when he knew something needed to change.

It's really weird to think about how so many good changes have happened in my life because really bad things happened to other people. It makes me feel a little guilty. I guess when you think about it, there are a lot of professions where this is true: doctors make more money when more people are sick, lawyers make more money when more illegal things happen; there are entire industries that run on cleaning up natural disasters or rebuilding cities after war. If everyone was well, if no one committed crimes, if natural disasters or war never happened, these people would be out of business. Yet I'm sure they don't wish for people to be sick or cities to be war-torn. Reporting is not much different. Sure, sometimes a reporter gets to tell good news. But when your main job is to cover crime, like it was for my dad, the majority of your business runs on tragedy.

So it was on the morning of December 14, 2012, when so many families' lives were about to be torn apart, that my family was about to be brought closer together. Less than two hours away from our home in Brooklyn, New York, a twenty-year-old boy named Adam Lanza woke up in his home in Newtown, Connecticut, and set out to bring destruction to his community. Adam first shot and killed his mother and then drove to Sandy Hook Elementary School, where he murdered twenty children and six adults. He then turned the gun on himself. In the span of just a few hours, twenty-eight people were killed, making it one of the deadliest mass shootings in US history.

That morning, my dad had just returned from another work trip. He said goodbye to us before we went to school, promising that we would spend some special time together when we got home. But life had other ideas. Shortly after sending us out the door, he got the call about Sandy Hook, and after only being back for a few hours, he had to rush out the door to Newtown, a place he would end up spending many weeks.

When I returned from school that day, I could tell something was wrong. As my mom pulled up to our house, I noticed my dad's car was gone and felt a sinking feeling inside my stomach. I assumed that was the reason my mom seemed so quiet and strange. I figured my dad had just been sent out of town for work again.

When we went inside, my mom told me and Izzy to sit down because she had something she needed to talk to us about. As she began to tell us what had happened at the Sandy Hook school, tears filled her eyes. I heard the words she was saying—*twenty children were killed*—but I just couldn't hold on to their meaning. I looked at Izzy for some idea of how to react. Izzy was tough. She never let things bother her the way I sometimes did. But even she looked stunned.

"So how long is Dad going to be gone this time?" Izzy asked, pulling herself together.

"I'm not sure, sweets, but I think this is going to be a long one."

8

THE BRIDGE

OVER THE NEXT FEW WEEKS, we saw my dad very little. It was Christmastime, and even though my mom made cookies with us and took us to see the lights in Dyker Heights, there was a hole where my dad usually was. It feels insensitive to complain about such a thing when so many families would never see their loved ones again. At least we would eventually have my dad back home. Still, I was six, and it was hard to think outside myself in that way.

Two hours away, my dad had the terrible job of attending the funerals of the children who were killed at Sandy Hook. Many of them were the same age as I was. When my dad looks back on this time, he tells us it was one of the most difficult things he has ever done. But there was a lesson in it for him—a lesson that would help glue our family back together. After interviewing almost all the parents of the children who had died, my dad found they all had the same regrets: that they hadn't appreciated the time they had together, that they took for granted that they would have all the moments in the world.

As a reporter, my dad always tried to remain objective—not influenced by personal feelings or opinions in considering and representing facts. But it was nearly impossible for him not to think of his own life—his own family he so often left behind. What if he didn't have endless moments with us? Would he have the same regrets as these families did? He knew he would.

The problem was my dad could not walk away from the biggest story in the country. Along with telling the victims' stories, there were many layers to investigate, from exactly what happened that day, to what had gone wrong with Adam Lanza, to how and if it could have been prevented. Not only was it truly important work, it was also how my dad financially supported our family of five. It wasn't enough to realize he needed to be home more. There needed to be some kind of bridge between what he was presently doing and the life he imagined where he wouldn't have to leave his family.

Luckily, my dad was a great reporter. During the many days he spent in Newtown, he was able to obtain exclusive e-mails that Nancy Lanza, Adam Lanza's mother, had sent and received. This communication helped to paint a more complete picture of just what went wrong with Adam. When something as tragic as the Sandy Hook shooting happens, people all have the same question: Why? The information my dad was able to get provided, at least somewhat, an answer to that question.

Keeping his goal of being home with his family in mind, my dad woke up extremely early every morning—sometimes at 3:00 AM—to begin working on a book proposal. A book proposal is a document designed to convince publishing houses to publish a book. It gives a brief summary of the main idea, sample chapters on the subject matter, and a marketing plan for the proposed book. He knew a great book could come from the exclusive information he gathered, but he had to race the clock to submit the book proposal before another reporter discovered what he had. Even then, there was no guarantee a publisher would buy his book idea. It was a risk he knew he needed to take. If he was successful, a book deal could provide enough money to help him transition away from the newspaper to writing from home.

He kept this a secret from all of us, even my mom. The mood of our house during those months felt really strange. On the one hand, we heard my dad say that he wanted to be home with us more. On the other hand, he continued to travel a lot for work, returning to Newtown many times, and he seemed to be gone more than he wasn't. Even though we all accepted this, our house felt much less happy than it had before.

In April, my mom decided to take us to spend some time visiting our grandparents in Pennsylvania. Looking back, I think the unhappiness caused by my dad's traveling was really getting to her. She was a nature girl like me and always felt better when she could hike in the fresh mountain air around where she grew up. We had been there for a few nights when we woke up one morning to hear a different voice coming from the dining room downstairs. At first we were confused because it sounded like my dad. Izzy and I wrote it off as wishful thinking and headed down in search of breakfast. But when we got to the bottom of the steps, we realized we weren't wrong—there, sitting at the table, was my dad!

What we didn't know was that he had driven to my grandparents' house from Brooklyn at two in the morning to surprise my mom. He had some very exciting news and could not wait another minute to tell her. He woke her up by calling her cell phone over and over. Once he reached her, he told her to throw some clothes on and meet him in the car out front. Nothing was open that late at night except a truck stop that had a diner inside. As soon as their coffee was poured, my dad told her the news:

"Our lives are about to change, Bridge," he began.

9

AN ADVENTURE

AFTER THE SURPRISE of seeing my dad at the breakfast table wore off, my parents told us to get dressed.

"We have some important things we need to talk to you about," my mom said.

The last time she had sat us down, we learned the terrible news about Sandy Hook, but looking at her face now, I saw no trace of sadness. In fact, both my parents were beaming with happiness. Izzy and I raced upstairs, threw on our dirty clothes from the day before, skipped brushing our teeth and hair, and flew right back down the steps in under two minutes. My mom must have been in some great mood, because she didn't make us march directly back upstairs to clean up.

After handing baby Georgie over to my grandmother Mimi, my mom rushed us out the door to my dad's car. Izzy and I had no idea what was going on. We felt a mixture of excitement and nervousness. When my dad made a left turn onto Route 11, we knew where he was headed. Riverlands was a nature preserve ten minutes from my Mimi's house that had hiking trails and a really cool playground. Izzy and I spent as much time there as we could when we came to visit.

But playing at Riverlands didn't seem to match the level of excitement my parents were displaying. And didn't they say they had something to tell us? My patience was wearing thin.

After what felt like an eternity, my dad pulled into the parking lot next to the playground. Izzy and I rushed out and grabbed our favorite swings. My parents joined us and took a seat on the ground right in front of us.

My mom began: "So, girls, life is about to get really interesting. Your dad has some very exciting news."

"I've been keeping a bit of a secret," he said. "I've been working on something, something to do with my job. And it's gone really well. I sold a book, girls. Well, not a book exactly. I still have to write the book. But the promise of a book. I sold it. For a lot of money."

Izzy and I both started jumping up and down and screaming. Honestly, we didn't really know what much of it meant, but the words "lot of money" combined with my parents' happiness made us feel like something magical was about to happen. And really, something was.

"So, this is all very exciting for me and my career, but it is most amazing because it means I'll be able to work from home now. I promised you guys I'd find a way, and I think this is it!"

At those words, my heart felt like it was going to explode. I could not believe that he would finally be able to be home with us. After the last six months of his constant travel, there was nothing more that Izzy and I could have wanted. And I know my mom felt the same.

"So, there's a little catch to it all," my mom said. "But I think it's going to be an exciting adventure. We are a family of adventurers, aren't we?"

Izzy and I were still kind of jumping around with all the good news. We nodded our heads to indicate that yes, of course, we were adventurers. Then, like in one of those television shows where the music stops suddenly and you hear the sound of brakes screeching, my mom said these next words:

"So, we are going to leave Brooklyn."

Say what now?

Seeing our faces freeze, my dad took over the conversation. "OK, here's the thing. This book deal—it's a lot of money, but not in terms of New York City. It's so expensive to live there. If I quit reporting for the *New York Daily News*, we couldn't live very long in Brooklyn on what the book is paying. But it is the kind of money that could buy us a nice big house somewhere else and allow me to be home with you guys while I write the book."

"So where are we going?" asked Izzy, most of the excitement gone from her voice.

"Well, that's the adventure," said my mom. "We don't know yet! Dad has four months to finish the book, and he's going to have to be in Newtown for most of that. I'm going to take you guys to Pennsylvania, and we will spend that time between Mimi and Pop-Pop's and Grammie and Grandpa's houses. The weather will be getting warm, and we can swim and play and spend time with everyone all while checking out places where we might want to move when Dad's done with the book."

"The beach," said Izzy, the joy returning to her voice. "We should move to the beach!"

My parents giggled and said that nothing was off limits. As Izzy began jumping up and down again, I felt some of my excitement return. But there was something else going on inside that I couldn't quite figure out. It wasn't that I was feeling bad about leaving Brooklyn—not yet at least. I replayed the last few minutes again in my mind and realized that the weird feeling came when I thought about my dad leaving the *Daily News*. It was everything we had been wishing for over the last six months, yet now that it was finally happening, I realized there was also a downside to his quitting the paper. Yes, he would be home with us now, but there would be no more reporting.

And if my dad wasn't reporting anymore, that meant *I* wouldn't be helping him report anymore. No more stakeouts or interviews. No more games of Elevators or Stairs. No exciting trips or helping catch bad guys. Even living at the beach seemed boring compared to reporting.

I told myself I was being crazy. I made myself think about how fun it would be to spend four months in Pennsylvania. I imagined living in a big house somewhere where my dad would always be sitting at the breakfast table in the morning. I looked at the happiness on the faces of my family members and decided to be happy too.

10

CHOCOLATE CHIP PANCAKES

THE FOUR MONTHS WE SPENT at my grandparents' houses were everything my mom had promised. We spent some of the time with my mom's mom, "Mimi," and Mom's grandfather, "Pop-Pop," and some of the time at the home of my dad's parents, "Grammie and Grandpa." The weather was warm, and it seemed everywhere we looked there were fields of green. We played outside, went to see my cousin's baseball games, and were all-around spoiled with games and sweet treats.

My dad rented a little cabin in Newtown, where he was writing the book. He came to stay with us on most weekends, but we were still in the familiar pattern of missing him. On one of his visits with us, I decided to tell him how I felt.

"I'm really glad you got the book deal, Dad, but it kind of stinks having you gone so much. Before, I could at least come to work with you."

That was all I had to say, because in a few short hours, Izzy and I found ourselves in the backseat of his car on our way to stay with him in Newtown. I was excited to get to spend time with him, but beyond that, I was really eager to see my dad in action again. I knew he was still doing a ton of interviews and constantly looking for new information about the shooting. Even though the story was so sad, I couldn't wait to go reporting with him again.

But when we got to the house my dad was renting, Izzy and I both had a little shock. Inside, my dad had taped a picture of every single victim of the shooting to the wall. He said it helped him stay focused and reminded him how important it was to tell the story of what had happened that day. The hope was that understanding it could prevent future tragedies. While it made sense to us, it did very little to quiet the creeped-out feeling we both had. The house was really just a tiny little cabin with a big open room. The bed we would be sleeping in was right under the wall of all the victims' pictures. Izzy and I looked at each other, neither one of us wanting to complain to our dad. Luckily, we didn't have to.

"I didn't know you guys would be coming back with me," my dad said as he carefully began removing the pictures one at a time.

Later that night, I woke to find my dad sitting at his desk. Izzy was sound asleep next to me. I watched him at his computer. He would type a few lines, then sit back and run his hands through his hair in frustration. I looked on quietly from the bed as he shuffled some papers around and pulled out the pictures he had taken off the wall earlier. He carefully arranged a few on his desk, stared at them for a long moment, and then began typing again. I fell back asleep to the sound of his fingers hitting the keys.

The next morning, I was so excited to go out reporting with my dad. I jumped out of bed as quickly as possible, afraid I had missed something. I could hear Izzy's feet crunching on the gravel outside. My dad was nowhere to be seen. I threw the screen door open and found my dad sipping his coffee on the front porch while Izzy searched for cool rocks to paint later on.

I was so relieved that he didn't leave without us.

"When are we going?" I asked.

"Oh, Hilds, I'm sorry. You guys aren't going to be able to go with me."

Seeing my face fall, he quickly added, "But I don't need to go any-where just yet. I thought we could go to breakfast first. If you promise not to tell Mom, you can have chocolate chips in your pancakes."

As much as I loved chocolate chip pancakes, I was so disappointed and confused. This was probably the biggest story my dad had ever covered. There would be so much for me to learn. I just didn't get it.

In the car on the way to the diner, my dad, sensing that I was bummed out, told me the reason that we couldn't go. It was something I had never even considered. "Hilds, I know you've been on some really serious stories with me, and I know you can handle it. It's not you I'm worried about, kiddo. It's the parents. I can't bring you with me when I interview them because you are the same age as the kids they just lost. Seeing you could be upsetting to *them*."

My heart sank into my stomach. I felt really dumb that it never crossed my mind to consider their feelings. I knew the families were in terrible amounts of pain. I just had never stopped to think about what it might be like for them when they went out into the world and had to see children—kids like me—alive and well. I realized there were bigger issues going on other than my own selfish desires. I was so lucky. All the members of our family were still with us, even if my dad traveled a lot. And after he finished the book, we'd never have to be separated again.

As we settled into the booth at the diner, I thought that on that day, eating a stack of warm chocolate chip pancakes with my dad and my sister was more than enough.

11

SETTLING IN

NOT LONG INTO OUR STAY WITH OUR GRANDPARENTS, it was decided, mainly by my mom, that we should begin looking to permanently settle in the area close to them. I was very happy about this. We had never lived near any of our relatives. The idea of being able to stop by to see my Mimi and Pop-Pop or Grammie and Grandpa whenever I wanted sounded like so much fun. Izzy wasn't as sold on the idea and used every opportunity to bring up how much more amazing life at the beach would be. My dad was just so happy to be finished with his book that he said he didn't care where we settled so long as we were all together.

I've since talked with my family members about how none of us could have known how life changing the decision to buy our house in Selinsgrove would be. I'm not sure what I think about fate or the idea that things are meant to happen as they do. But as I look back, one thing is for sure: I wouldn't be sitting here writing this book had my mom given in to Izzy and moved us to the beach.

Selinsgrove, Pennsylvania, is a small town of around five thousand people about an hour south of the state capital of Harrisburg. It is about a half-hour drive to Danville, where my Grammie and Grandpa lived, and an hour from my Mimi and Pop-Pop in Berwick. The Susquehanna River runs along each of these towns but is particularly beautiful when it hits Selinsgrove. There are trees everywhere, and in the spring and summer you can walk in the soft green grass on the riverbanks and see flowers growing wild.

Having lived in tiny apartments in Brooklyn for so long, my mom was desperate to have a big house with lots of outdoor space. My dad just wanted to be walking distance to a coffee shop and have room for a firepit outside somewhere. My mom was also in love with old things that had what she referred to as "character." I never really understood what she meant by that until the first time I laid eyes on our new house in Selinsgrove. It definitely seemed to have a personality all its own. First of all, it was gigantic. In Brooklyn, four families could have easily shared the space! And it was old—over one hundred years old, in fact. Because of this, there were really interesting details like pocket doors, hardwood floors, a library, and two separate staircases. Apparently, when the house was built, the back staircase was for the hired help. My mom liked to make jokes that she was the hired help now. The third-floor attic was completely finished and had its own bathroom. Izzy and I claimed this area as our own. Because it was right under the roof, the ceilings were pointed almost like a triangle. This made comfy little nooks for each of our beds.

True to his word, after finishing his book, *Newtown: An American Tragedy*, my dad quit his job at the *New York Daily News*. He was always downstairs drinking coffee with my mom when I woke up and home to tuck me and my sisters in to bed each night. When school began a month after we moved in, I would walk the two blocks by myself in the morning, but most days he would walk to meet me on my way home. The mood in our house was so much lighter and happier than that last year we had lived in Brooklyn.

A joyful Hilde, six, with her sisters, Izzy, nine, and Georgia, two, on the day they moved to Selinsgrove, Pennsylvania.

We also happened to move to a block that was full of girls. That summer, we counted seven between the ages of me and Izzy. Izzy fell in fast with the girls her age, and I played for a while with one of their sisters. But we didn't seem to be a great match for each other. We were just into different things. At school, I talked to most of the kids in my class and even hung out with a few, but overall I was still a little lonely. Izzy and I had amazing friends, Charlotte and Arabelle, in Brooklyn. Charlotte was Izzy's age and Arabelle, her sister, was a year older than I was. We had played together since I was a baby. Even though we visited them, and they us, and despite hanging out with the girls on our block, something seemed to be missing.

Then I met Kristen. Well, first I met her annoying little brother, Joey. Joey was in my class at school and was the kind of kid who wore raccoon fur hats and always had some type of toy gun at his side. He would knock on our door and ask to play, and my mom would let him in despite the fact that he always kind of freaked me out. I would be playing Barbies in my room and he would try to turn whatever story I had created into something involving war. Not exactly my idea of fun.

One day, Joey's mom sent Kristen to our house to bring him home. Because she was just a year older than Izzy, my mom, always trying to matchmake us with friends, invited Kristen in to hang out. Looking back at that moment, I have to laugh to myself. There may be no worse friend match on the planet than Kristen and Izzy. Kristen is what my grandmother would call "quirky," a word that means kind of strange, but not necessarily in a bad way. At eleven, Kristen still liked to play dress-up and would often be out and about in a tutu or some other elaborate costume. She cut her hair short if she felt like it, usually all by herself, and could be seen still playing with toys on her front porch, which was directly across the street from ours.

Izzy, on the other hand, was "cool." She was the type of girl who seemed to do everything that everyone wanted to do, from the way she dressed to the things she did in her free time. She had never really liked to play with toys when she was younger, and by the age of ten, she had given up on them entirely, preferring instead to write songs or go shopping. When Kristen and Izzy hung out that first day, there wasn't exactly awkward silence because Kristen talks nonstop, but it was definitely awkward. Still, Kristen never seemed bothered by that, and she came back the next day.

The next time she came back to our house, Izzy wasn't home. My mom invited her in to wait. When she came upstairs to our bedroom, I was there playing with Barbies. After admiring my favorite Barbie house, she asked if she could play. The rest is history. We played together that day and most every day after that until my family moved out of Selinsgrove almost six years later.

12

TUESDAY NIGHTS

THE FIRST YEAR IN SELINSGROVE—the year I turned seven—was pretty wonderful. I mostly enjoyed school, played with Kristen, chilled in my room, and hung out with my family.

One of the absolute best things was Tuesday nights. Every Tuesday, Izzy had a guitar lesson in the town where my Grammie and Grandpa lived. We would drop her off and go visit with my grandparents. My Grammie was pretty obsessed with food and eating, so immediately after we arrived, she would sit us on the barstools in her kitchen and begin feeding us snacks. Cookies, pastries, ice cream bars—you name it, she had it. This drove my mom, who was super obsessed with healthy eating, totally crazy. But my Grammie was very convincing. She had a BIG, vibrant personality and made every single thing she did seem like so much fun. She and my mom were very close friends. And even though they didn't share the same ideas about junk food, my mom didn't stand a chance against my Grammie's sweet treats. Grammie won out every time.

When Izzy was back from her guitar lesson, we would sit at Grammie's big dining room table with my Grandpa, my uncle Andy and aunt Keri, and my cousin Boo for a big delicious (usually Italian) meal. There was always dessert and coffee afterward while the adults lingered and we played in the other room.

My Grandpa was a professor of history at the local college. He loved reading and studying. He also had a photographic memory. We could pick any book off his shelf, turn to a random page, and begin reading a sentence, and he could finish it exactly. He wasn't the most talkative person—that title would always go to my Grammie—but he would hang around as long as the conversation was interesting. We always knew when Grandpa was bored after dinner because he would get up without saying a word and go into his study, where he would read and listen to classical music.

It would be dark when we made the half-hour drive back to Selinsgrove. With our bellies full and the car all warm and toasty, my sisters would often fall asleep before we made it home. I've never been able to sleep in the car, but I would look out the window as my parents' voices faded in the front seat and think just how happy I was. There was no way to know how limited those Tuesday nights would be, but I like to think we all appreciated them as much as possible.

One Tuesday night, my parents said we were going to leave a little early. My dad said he had a surprise for us. My dad is famous for his surprises—they could be anything from "Pack your bag—we're leaving on a trip in an hour" to "Go look in my car," where we would find a new pet. We never knew quite what to expect. So when he pulled into a car dealership in Grammie and Grandpa's town, we just assumed we'd be getting a new car. But that was the least of the surprise.

After what felt like three million hours later, we were all buckled into our new Chevrolet Traverse, heading to Grammie and Grandpa's. The car was nice—there was a third row of seats, so Izzy and I didn't have to be smooshed into the second row with Georgie's car seat anymore. It was definitely an improvement, but not as good as a trip to the beach or a puppy.

About a mile from my grandparents' house, my mom turned the music down. "So, girls," she began, "there's a reason we bought this car today."

I really didn't know what to think. I thought maybe we were going to get some ice cream or take that trip after all. Georgie was two years old now and had an impressive amount of stuff we had to lug around. Our next family vacation would be very uncomfortable in the old car. So as I was imagining all the different places we could travel to—maybe California since I had never seen the West Coast— my mom said these words: "Our family is about to get bigger. We're going to have another baby!"

It was all I could do to not barf all over the third row of our brand-new car.

I've thought about this moment many times since. My mom and I have talked about it a lot. Still, I have no idea why my mom having another baby felt so horrible to me. It's not like I was the baby anymore. It seems like it would have made sense for me to be upset about Georgie's birth. I was younger and used to being the littlest. But that never bothered me. For some strange reason, this did. I remember my stomach felt like an elevator crashing to the ground as Izzy began cheering. Something I've always found to be out of character for Izzy is how excited she is when my mom is pregnant. For someone who isn't very emotional or cuddly, Izzy loves babies. In the car that day, I tried hard to put a smile on my face, as Izzy was screaming with joy and trying to explain to Georgie that she was going to be a big sister. No one really noticed the dread I felt.

I kept my feelings to myself during dinner at Grammie and Grandpa's. I sat quietly, eating only the croutons out of my salad as everyone gushed about my mom's pregnancy. Already there was talk that maybe this one would be a boy. My parents never cared about that stuff, but it seemed to be a big deal to other people. Even strangers, when seeing my mom with her three daughters, would say, "Trying for the boy next?" It all made me feel kind of gross.

Over the next few months, my mom's belly grew and she began to take naps in the afternoons. My dad was still home all the time, working on a new book. I wasn't feeling quite as upset about the baby anymore. I just didn't feel as happy as before. And I was getting bored of my routine. I loved having a big house and being close to my grandparents, but I missed the hustle and bustle of New York City. In our old neighborhood in Brooklyn, there were tons of coffee shops and restaurants on every block. In Selinsgrove, the downtown was one block long and had only one or two places to go. I took advantage of riding my bike to the local coffee shop, the Kind Cafe, and browsing in the Mustard Seed (a thrift shop I loved), but that only passed so much time.

What I really missed was going reporting with my dad. Kristen would go along with playing journalist Barbie games for only so long. I was sick of playing. I needed something real and exciting. Maybe there wasn't much in the way of excitement happening in my life, but there were real things. Maybe I didn't need my dad after all. I grabbed a red crayon and set to work.

13

THE *SOME TIMES*

I DIDN'T EVEN STOP when my hand cramped up. I had been writing for over an hour, with only a short break to go interview my mom. After my story was all written down in red crayon, I stopped for a long moment to think of a title for my new newspaper. At this point, I wasn't sure how often I would be able to put a copy out, so I didn't want to name it something with "daily" in the title, like the *New York Daily News* had. Since the paper was going to cover news for my family, I thought about using our name, but Lysiak wasn't exactly catchy. When I thought more about how often I would be able to put a newspaper out, the answer I came up with was "sometimes." Then it hit me—the *Some Times*! My seven-year-old self thought it was very clever.

The next thing I had to do was make a copy for each member of my family. After the last word was written, I shook my aching hand out, put down my crayon, and set off to find my family.

"Family announcement!" I shouted.

Family announcements were taken very seriously in my house. Any member could call one, but it had better be for something that didn't waste the other members' time. (I learned this the hard way when I called a family announcement to tell everyone my favorite doll was going to have a baby.) Today I was sure of myself. I had something really good.

My mom and dad, Izzy, and Georgie were all crammed onto the couch in our living room. As I handed each of them a copy of the *Some Times*, I watched as my dad's face lit up.

"Exclusive! Mom Gets New Car," he said, reading my headline out loud.

Since I had interviewed my mom for the story, she probably wasn't very surprised, but she did a good job of faking it.

"Hilde! This is so great! I can't believe you did all this by yourself!" she said.

"I can," my dad answered. "This one's got reporter's blood in her."

I handed out my next issue four days later. This time, I wrote about my mom being pregnant. I interviewed Georgie about how she felt about becoming a big sister. I was careful to leave my feelings out of the story. Although the unhappiness I felt probably would have been news to my family, I remembered my dad's lesson on staying objective.

A few days later, when I picked up another crayon and began writing the next issue of the *Some Times*, I began to feel silly. What was I doing? Whatever it was didn't feel like real journalism. It felt more like a baby paper: something that adults could smile about but that no one took seriously. How could anyone respect a paper written in crayon? I knew I could do real reporting, but making it look legitimate was another matter.

I knocked on the door to my dad's office. "Hey, Dad, I need to talk to you about something," I said.

He made a noise that meant I could come in. He was still staring at the screen of his computer when I walked through the door. It was his writing face. That meant I only had a quarter of his attention, at most.

"I want to do real reporting. You know, like we used to do," I said.

"That's great," he answered, his eyes still glued to the screen.

"I can do it all myself, I just need some help making it look real," I added.

"Great," he repeated.

I bit my lower lip. I could feel the anger rising up from my toes. "DAD!"

It came out louder than I had meant it to, but at least my dad finally looked up, his eyes wide. I had his attention.

"I want to do my own newspaper and not a baby one with crayon, but I don't know how and I need help making it look real," I repeated.

My dad looked me in the eye. He knew I was serious. "As you know, reporting can be a lot of hard work," he said. "If you decide you really want to run your own newspaper, I will help you with the layout and printing, but you would have to do all the reporting and take all the pictures."

I didn't need to think it over. Writing those stories was the most excitement I had felt since we left Brooklyn. Since then, I had been trying to come up with more ideas, but not that much was happening in my family at the moment. It also occurred to me that I wasn't exactly giving them news they didn't already know.

"Deal!" I told my dad. "But I don't know if I'll have enough interesting stuff if I just cover our family."

"Well, why does it have to cover just our family?"

14

THE *ORANGE STREET NEWS*

───────

S HORTLY AFTER MOVING TO ORANGE STREET IN SELINSGROVE, we became close friends with our neighbors, the Groces. Sue and Brian were a bit older than my parents and had a teenage daughter, Maggie. They also had an awesome swimming pool that they invited us to use all the time. My family spent many late summer afternoons there. My parents would chat with Sue and Brian, and Maggie would play games with us while we swam. She even babysat for us sometimes.

That summer—the summer of 2014—I had taken my dad's advice and decided not to limit my newspaper to our family. Because I would be branching out of our house, I chose to release the newest version of my paper once a month. This gave me time to find story ideas and arrange interviews, as well as the freedom to publish more than one story per issue. After many suggestions from friends and family, I decided to call the paper the *Orange Street News*. My aunt Keri almost talked me into naming it the *Hilde Herald* because it sounded cool, but in the end, I didn't want the paper to be about me. It was all very exciting.

It was also incredibly overwhelming. How would I get enough stories to fill an entire issue? Who would even want to read it? What if it totally stank? What if I couldn't do it at all? I imagined going up to my dad and telling him that I had failed. Even though I knew my dad wouldn't be disappointed in me, how could I ever tell the best reporter I knew that I wasn't able to do it? The thought of it made me want to die of embarrassment.

Since those early days, I've been in many high-pressure situations. What I've learned is that it's OK to allow yourself a moment to freak out. The key is you just can't get stuck there. You need to acknowledge that you're afraid and then move on. My mom has always told us, "Being brave doesn't mean you're not afraid. Being brave is feeling that fear and doing it anyway." If I hadn't listened to her, my paper would have died with that last paper copy written in red crayon.

One evening in September, we were sitting outside of Brian and Sue's house. They always made a big deal of celebrating before they closed the pool for the season. Maggie, who had gone to college for the first time in August, was even back for the weekend. I still had my newspaper on my mind and was zoning in and out of the adults' conversation when I heard something I found interesting.

"It's super gross—I literally have to shower with shoes on," Maggie was saying.

"What?" I asked, snapping to attention. "Why?"

As Maggie began to explain the various foot fungi that existed in the bathroom of her college dorm, it occurred to me that she had already answered three of the five important questions a reporter should ask. Maybe you've heard of them? Sometimes called the Five W's—*who, what, where, when,* and *why*—they are questions that when answered will give a complete idea of something that has happened. They can be used to understand books or movies; they're especially helpful when trying to solve a mystery, and as my dad taught me early on, they are the backbone of any good news story.

The three W's I already knew that day at the Groces' pool were:

- **Who:** Maggie Groce
- **What:** Students at Maggie's college have to shower with shoes on
- **Why:** College dorm bathrooms are disgusting and gross

Even though I knew that Maggie was "away at college," I didn't know exactly *where* that was. To get that fourth W, I just needed to ask for the name of the college she attended and where it was located. The last W, the *when*, was also pretty easy—according to Maggie, "All the time!"

There was something else that was very important to do. Another lesson my dad taught me that first day I went out reporting with him was that you always have to introduce yourself as a reporter before you start asking questions. Not everyone wants their name in the newspaper. By introducing yourself as a reporter, you give the person an opportunity to say whether they want to talk to you. That is the person's right. As Maggie went into more detail, I knew I had to stop her.

"For real . . . this girl I knew two doors down forgot her flip-flops and literally all the skin is peeling off her feet—" Maggie was saying.

"Sorry to interrupt," I interrupted. "But I'm putting together a newspaper, and I'm wondering if I can use this for one of my stories?"

Maggie laughed. I'm not sure if it was because she thought I was silly and cute (something I would never get used to) or if the idea of talking about foot fungus for a newspaper was funny. The most important part was that after she laughed, she said yes.

I pulled out my small blue notepad and pen and quickly began writing down everything Maggie had just told me, being extra careful to write her words exactly as she said them. It wasn't easy! When I was just listening, I felt like I had a handle on the interview. It wasn't much different from a conversation. I just had to be especially curious. But when it came to having to listen and ask questions while writing everything down, I felt like my brain might explode! I had to stop a few times and ask Maggie to repeat herself. It made me feel like I wasn't doing the best job, but I told myself to just keep going.

The next afternoon, my dad called me into his office. "I thought you might like to use my computer to type out your story," he said. "You can sit at my desk, if you'd like, so that you can have your privacy."

When I think back, we had no way of knowing how many hours upon hours I would end up spending at that desk. So many, in fact, that my dad would let me hang an ORANGE STREET NEWS sign on the door.

But first, I had to get more stories to complete my first issue. And things were about to get very interesting.

Hilde in action, reporting on construction in Selinsgrove.

15

"THE WORST DAY
OF MY LIFE"

S O MAYBE "INTERESTING" is a bit misleading. Most people probably think of interesting as something good. A reporter thinks differently. Like I mentioned before, some of the best news is actually very sad. Unfortunately, as I was in the exciting process of completing my first issue of the *Orange Street News*, things were about to take a turn for the worse.

First of all, as my eighth birthday approached, my mom still hadn't had the baby. Izzy's birthday was October 30, the day before Halloween, and my birthday was November 2, just two days after Halloween. Izzy didn't want to share her birthday with the new baby. Neither of us wanted her (yep, another girl—everyone was wrong again) to be born on Halloween. My birthday party was scheduled for the day before my birthday, so I didn't want her coming then, and of course not the next day on my birthday. So as I dressed in my scary Elsa costume (basically my answer to the question, *What would happen if Elsa from* Frozen *got attacked by an ax murderer?* . . . It seemed like a good idea at the time . . .), I wished my hardest for my mom to stay pregnant for at least three more days.

But then it happened. My mom's water broke.

Looking back, I feel like such a brat. My poor mom was gigantic and so uncomfortable. The baby was already almost two weeks late. I can't imagine what upset me so much or made me act so selfishly, but all I know is my only thought was, *This is going to ruin trick-or-treating!*

Then I overheard my parents talking.

"No, take them, Matt. This isn't our first time around. You know it's going to be hours before the baby comes. There's no need to rush anywhere," my mom was saying.

"But the midwife said it could happen really fast since it's our fourth baby. I just don't think it's a good idea to take them trick-or-treating," my dad said.

"Go. I promise I'll call you if anything changes. My contractions aren't even that strong now. We've got time."

I had never loved my mom more than in that moment. I was bummed that she couldn't come trick-or-treating with us but was so happy she was able to convince my dad to take us. But somewhere between the joy of stealing all of Georgie's Butterfingers when she wasn't looking and the freezing walk back toward our house, the feeling of dread crept back in.

The next morning was my birthday party. Usually I liked to have a low-key day with my family—maybe go see a movie, go out to dinner, that kind of thing. This year, though, I had decided I wanted to do something bigger. After much consideration, it seemed like a roller-skating party was the perfect thing. I had invited everyone in my class as well as Kristen. But as we made our way back into the house from trick-or-treating, I could tell right away the baby was coming sooner rather than later. With only a few hours until the party, I started to think it wasn't going to happen.

When we got home, my Mimi and Pop-Pop were there. My mom was pacing back and forth, stopping every few minutes in obvious pain. My parents weren't going to have the baby in a hospital, but they did need to drive thirty minutes to their midwife's house. My mom's bag was already by the door. I wasn't surprised when she told my dad she thought it was time to go.

Juliet Poe Lysiak was born November 1 at 3:00 AM. Both she and my mom were completely healthy. My Mimi and Pop-Pop stayed with us overnight, but none of us got much sleep—them from excitement, me from worry about my party. But, as it turned out, my parents were home with baby Juliet by 7:00 AM—three hours before it started.

We have a tradition in our family that the next-oldest sister gets to hold the new baby first. She is considered that baby's "protector." When I saw Georgie, who was just three, hold Juliet for the first time, I have to admit, something in me softened. She was so excited to be a big sister. It reminded me of how I felt when she was born. I wondered again what had happened to make me feel so differently this time. Was I just a jerk now? I really hoped not.

Four hours later I sat in the restaurant area of the skating rink, hating life. My mom, of course, stayed home with the baby, but my dad was able to come. Unfortunately, neither of us really knew my skate size, so my feet were killing me from wearing the wrong ones. To make matters worse, only three people came, and one of them was throwing a temper tantrum at the moment because she didn't like the pizza the rink was serving.

Luckily, Izzy was there. Even though the pizza-hating kid was making me miserable, I was too polite to skate away. Izzy, on the other hand, is never worried about those kinds of manners. Her top priority was that I have fun at my birthday party. As Meghan Trainor's "All About That Bass," boomed from the speakers, Izzy grabbed my hand and pulled me out onto the skating rink. Neither of us was very good, but we laughed our heads off each time we fell.

The next day my mom still managed to make me a birthday cake, and we had a quiet little celebration at home. My Grammie and Grandpa were there dropping off food (of course!) so my mom wouldn't have to worry about dinner. I tried my hardest to act happy as I blew out my candles and opened my presents, but my mood was still unusually low.

One of my gifts was a pretty little notebook with handmade paper. I decided to use it as a diary. On the first page I wrote:

Today is my 8th birthday. It is the worst day of my life.

I know I'm supposed to laugh about this—oh what a silly, dramatic kid I was!—but this is a memory that has not been edited by time or other people's perspectives. That day *was* the worst day of my life—at least at that point, anyway. In just a few weeks, I would learn just how much worse things could get.

16

THE FIRST ISSUE

―――――――

M Y MAMMY WOULD SOMETIMES TALK ABOUT "the calm before the storm."
Probably a lot of people's grandmothers used this expression. It
means that something crazy or bad is about to happen, but like right
before a thunderstorm, there is period of calm. The month after I
turned eight could be explained that way. I felt a little better once
my birthday was over.

It helped that I had something exciting to focus on as I finished
the first edition of the *Orange Street News*. I decided that even though
the new baby was a bit of a bummer for me, it was a great cover story
for the paper. When people call me a "genius" or a "child prodigy"
for starting my own newspaper, I think back to that first edition and
laugh. Someone having a perfectly healthy baby was hardly hard news.
But I was learning. And I imagined that most of the neighbors on
Orange Street would find it interesting.

My dad and I stuck to that deal we had made in his room all
those weeks earlier and would keep for all the years I published the
Orange Street News. I did all the reporting and writing; he did the layout and the formatting. This didn't mean that I was without help. My

dad was a mentor to me. As someone who had successfully done what I was attempting to do, my dad would give me tips and advice that had worked for him. One of the most helpful things was a handwritten template he came up with for how to write a news story. My dad explained to me that even the most complicated article still followed this basic structure:

- **Lede:** This is the catchy introduction to the story that is supposed to grab the readers' attention and make them want to keep reading. According to my dad, the best ledes are short—ideally, one sentence.
- **Nut:** This is where those Five W's should be answered. Any of the who, what, where, when, and whys that are not in the lede need to be addressed here.
- **Quote:** This is where you put the exact words of someone you interviewed that are important to the story. Whereas the rest of the article should be straightforward without anything flashy, the quote is different. It is the one opportunity to really give color to your story while moving it along. For example, in a crime story, everything besides the quote should be facts. However, a quote like, "I was staring down the barrel of the gun watching my life flash before my eyes" brings emotion and interest to the article while also moving the story forward.
- **Support:** This is a place for additional information that isn't as important as what you put in the nut. A news story should be like an upside-down pyramid with the most important information at the top and the least important toward the bottom. The support is the place for facts that add interest to the story. For example, if the article is about a lost dog, the Five W's would have already been answered in the lede and the nut. The reader would know who the dog belonged to, what kind of dog it is, where it was last seen, when it went missing, and why it got loose in the first place. A good support might then be, "This is the third time the dog has run away this year." This isn't crucial to the story, but it does add something more intriguing.

- **Kicker:** This can be a call to action or a quote that makes the reader want to get the next issue of the paper. For example, in a crime story, a kicker that is a call to action might say, "If anyone has any information on the robber's identity, please call . . ." In the case of the lost dog story, the kicker might be a quote from the dog's owner that says, "I don't know how I'll be able to live without my dog!" This makes the reader want to check back in on the next issue of the paper to find out what happened: *Did they find the dog? How is the owner surviving without it?*

So when I sat down to begin writing my very first full issue of the *Orange Street News*, I had all my notes from the interviews I had done spread out on my dad's desk, along with the template my dad made. It was tricky at first to figure out how to arrange all the information properly. My first handwritten copies didn't follow this format at all—I just wrote the information like I was talking to someone. Doing it the right way took more time, but it felt good to take all the information I gathered and organize it in a way that made the most sense for the readers.

On December 1, 2014, from a little home printer in my dad's office, the very first issue of the *Orange Street News* was born. That first copy was one folded page that contained four stories and a short "Message from Hilde," where I introduced myself as the publisher of the paper.

I've gone on to do some pretty awesome things, but nothing I have experienced could top how I felt that day holding my very first issue. There had been moments of great doubt along the way, but I pushed through. I felt so proud of myself!

But somewhere off in the distance, the storm was brewing.

ORANGE STREET NEWS

Premier Edition | December

LOOK INSIDE:

Stray Cats Find Home on Orange

Two new stray cat were found wondering on Orange Street, sources tell the News.

Local Girl Featured on WKOK Radio

Sixth grade Orange Street girl makes first live media appearance!

INTERVIEW: Maggie Groce

On leaving home, dorms, and what college is *really* like. EXCLUSIVE INTERVIEW INSIDE

Orange Street Woman Hits Right Note!

Receives flowers from friends for Bucknell performance.

A Special Exclusive Offer Inside!

Find out how to get your subscription to the Orange Street News at the unbelievable price of $1 for a

New Baby on Orange Street
Juliet Poe Lysiak was born on November 1st
EXCLUSIVE FIRST PICTURE!

By Hilde Kate Lysiak

Bridget Lysiak and Matthew Lysiak were just getting ready to go trick-or-treating when Bridget's water broke. At 3 am Saturday, November 1 she had the baby. Her name is Juliet Poe Lysiak. She had the baby at a midwife farm in Mifflinburg.

"We had the baby because we love the children we have and wanted to have more," Bridget Lysiak told the News.

Juliet Poe Lysiak is a good baby so far and sleeps very well.

"A happy baby, sleeping through the nights," said Bridget.

Juliet Lysiak's birth makes the cover of the first issue of the *Orange Street News*.

17

GATHERING SPEED

———

A FULL DAY WENT BY where I rode on the happiness of my success. The next day was Tuesday, and I couldn't wait to bring a copy of the *Orange Street News* to my Grammie and Grandpa's house for dinner. Even though my Grammie acted very excited for me, something seemed off at their house. But I was so wrapped up in my paper, it wouldn't be until after dinner that I realized what was going on.

In the meantime, my Grammie insisted on paying me for my paper. Eventually I wanted to begin charging money for a subscription, but it seemed too soon. I thought about those grocery trips to Fairway in Brooklyn with my mom and how the store always had people passing out yummy samples of food for free. Of course, if it tasted good, people would end up buying it, even if it wasn't on their list. I thought I would use a similar plan. The next day, I would knock on the doors of every house on my block, handing out a free copy. If I gave them something good enough, eventually they'd want to buy it. But as Grammie shoved two dollars in my hand, who was I to resist? Her one condition was that I keep writing.

I figured two dollars was a pretty good price for a year's subscription. It also put a little pressure on me to keep reporting. If I agreed to Grammie's deal, I would owe her an issue each month. I decided to accept. Grammie then proceeded to buy four more subscriptions—one for each of my uncles and two for her friends—and then called us to the table for dinner.

If I was paying attention during the meal, I would have noticed that my Grandpa didn't eat. I would have seen that he looked much thinner than the last time I saw him. The sound of Grammie's leg jumping up and down under the table (something she did when she was nervous) would have bothered me. But I was busy planning which doors I would knock on first the next day.

After the dishes were cleared and Izzy and I were hanging out with Boo in the other room, I overheard something that caught my attention: "The family doctor says it's not back, but I just don't understand—look at him—he's so thin and frail, he's not eating, and he hasn't taken his walk in weeks," my Grammie was saying to my mom and dad and aunt and uncle.

"Mom, relax. It's probably nothing. I mean, he's getting older. It's probably not crazy for him to slow down," my dad said.

"I think we need to make an appointment with the oncologist to be sure," Grammie answered.

Five years before this, my Grandpa was diagnosed with a type of cancer called mantle cell lymphoma. He went through chemotherapy and had a bone marrow transplant. Although the treatment almost killed him, it ended up working, and there was no more cancer in his body. The doctors did tell my Grammie, though, that the cancer had a high likelihood of returning. As I sat in the other room eavesdropping, I understood that my Grammie thought the cancer was back.

On the way home, my parents were doing this weird thing when they don't want us to know what they're talking about. When Izzy and I were younger, they would spell words out, but that wouldn't work anymore. Now they had a weird kind of code that involved using people's initials instead of names and omitting certain words while they made really intense eye contact. It was kind of bizarre to watch, and also pretty ineffective. As my sisters slept, I listened carefully and was able to deduce that my mom shared my Grammie's concern that the cancer had returned in Grandpa. My dad, on the other hand, seemed to think that was crazy.

My mom has often said that a person's best quality can also be their worst. This sounds backward and confusing, but when I think about my dad, I understand better. One of his best qualities is that he is an optimist. That is a fancy word for someone who always believes the best thing will happen. This means he usually has an upbeat attitude and doesn't think anything is out of reach. I think one of the reasons he works so hard is that he believes anything is possible if you just put your mind and energy toward it. The downside of this is that sometimes bad things happen and there is nothing you can do to prevent them, no matter how much you hope or how hard you work. Being an optimist means you might have a big shock when those bad things happen.

Riding in the car that night, I wasn't sure what to believe, but as I thought back about how my Grandpa was at dinner, I started to worry.

18

"WHERE ARE YOUR PARENTS?"

I DIDN'T SLEEP MUCH or well that night. When I finally opened my eyes the next morning, the thought of passing out my paper replaced some of the worry that had made me toss and turn all evening. I jumped out of bed, got dressed, and grabbed fifteen copies of the *Orange Street News* from my dad's office. As I was leaving, I ran into my dad in the hallway.

"Hey, kiddo. Off to pass out your paper?"

"Yep!" I said as I dropped half of them on the floor.

My dad laughed. "Come with me, Hilds."

I followed him back into his office, where he handed me a canvas *New Yorker* tote bag.

"Why don't you use this?" he asked. "And here," he said, handing me five dollars. "Why don't you stop by the Kind Cafe for a bagel and a tea?"

"Actually," I said, as an idea struck me. "Do you think I could put some papers there?"

"Hilds, that is a great idea!" my dad said. "You'd better grab some more copies."

Forty minutes later, with a full belly and five copies of the *Orange Street News* on the reading shelf at the Kind Cafe, I began knocking on the doors on my block. Most of the neighbors were very excited to accept an issue. But I was about to find out not everyone supported what I was doing. This would be my first small taste of bigger problems I would encounter later on.

There is a lesson to learn when dealing with the public. It seems very simple but can be much harder than it sounds: *don't care what they think about you.* Of course, I wanted everyone to love my paper. But I was also prepared that some people wouldn't. If that was the case, I knew I would just have to work harder and get better. What I wasn't prepared for were all the opinions people would have *about me.*

On the more harmless yet annoying side were comments like this:

"Well, aren't you just adorable!"

"Look, honey, this cutie-pie is handing out a little newsletter."

"Well, well, well . . . what do we have here? Are you selling Girl Scout Cookies?"

Even though these people were speaking out of kindness, I still felt annoyed. I wanted desperately to be taken seriously. I wanted people to read my paper because they wanted the news, not because they thought it was adorable that an eight-year-old would put together a "little" paper. I also had to wonder if they would be saying those things if I were a boy. Still, I tucked my feelings inside and carried on with my door knocks. Then I began hearing things like:

"Where are your parents?"

"It's not safe for you to be walking around by yourself."

"No, I don't want your newspaper. You should be home playing, not out roaming the neighborhood."

This was so confusing to me. Izzy and I had lived in the biggest city in the country and were allowed to walk around our block by ourselves. Our parents always taught us that if anything ever happened—if we ever felt unsafe—to go into a store and tell an adult. But now it seemed as if many of the adults were afraid. I did not understand the world to be the dangerous place they spoke of. Sure, I had seen a lot of crime while reporting with my dad. That just made me realize how fortunate I was to live in places where there were no gangs or big drug problems, where people weren't struggling in poverty or living on the streets. I knew many of my neighbors and would have no problem going to them if I felt in danger, just as I had felt comfortable going to an adult in a business back in my Brooklyn neighborhood. But in all the days I had spent riding my bike or walking around by myself, I never once felt scared. It seemed silly that I would start feeling fear now in a small town of five thousand whose biggest recent crime was teenagers stealing change out of unlocked cars.

I also didn't like that people were criticizing my parents. This would be something we'd all get very used to (to the point of boredom, really) in the coming years, but this was the first time anyone had ever suggested my parents were anything besides awesome. Sure, they annoyed me sometimes, but I was so appreciative of the space they gave us. I may have been one of the only eight-year-olds to be able to ride my bike around town by myself, and without that freedom I doubt there ever would have been an *Orange Street News*.

When I made it back to my house two hours later, my parents were in the living room. Georgie, now incredibly graceful at three, was performing one of her choreographed dances as baby Juju lay on a blanket nearby. My parents looked like they were in the middle of another intense conversation but rearranged their faces into joy when they saw me. I spent the next ten minutes filling them in on my adventure. When I got to the part about the critical neighbors, my mom got really angry.

"Which neighbors?" she wanted to know right away.

My mom is one of the kindest people you could ever meet. She is very friendly and always concerned about making other people feel comfortable. Just don't mess with her kids. People are often shocked by the side of her personality that comes out when defending her children. It takes a lot to push her there, but when it happens—look out. She doesn't yell (which is probably even scarier than yelling). Instead, she gets like one of those TV lawyers who tears the witness to shreds.

Since we were still new to the neighborhood, I started to regret telling my mom anything about the neighbors who gave me a hard time. The last thing I wanted was her going to their houses to "have a little talk" with them. If I was going to be taken seriously as a reporter, I had to learn to fight my own battles, and this one didn't seem worth bothering with.

Luckily, it was possible to persuade my mom not to confront the neighbors. After all, people were allowed to have their own opinions about our family, even if we didn't agree with them. My parents were also distracted by several things. With Christmas right around the corner, there were constantly things to be done. My dad, still trying to make up for having missed so much of Christmas that last year in Brooklyn, went all out. Instead of going to a tree stand for our Christmas tree, we now went out into the woods and cut down our own. Every night, he would put me and Georgie into a wagon (Izzy was already "too cool" for this) and pull us around the neighborhood to look at all the pretty lights. There were Christmas movies to watch, cookies to bake, and trips to see Santa. Meanwhile, my mom decorated our house and spent what seemed like weeks cooking all the special foods we would eat on Christmas Eve.

There were also more trips to my Grammie and Grandpa's house. It seemed like we were going a few days a week now. Instead of eating a big meal each time we went, the grown-ups would send us into another room to play while they sat in the living room talking in hushed voices. My Grandpa spent much of this time in his recliner in his study, just listening to classical music. He wasn't doing any better. In fact, he seemed worse each time we visited.

I kept from worrying about my Grandpa so much by working on the next issue of the *Orange Street News*. But just like Grammie used to say, it's never the things you're worrying about. I had no way of knowing how right she was.

19

THE LAST

DO YOU EVER WISH you knew when something was the last? The last time you would want to play with your favorite childhood toy, the last time your older sibling would think you were cool, the last time you would have to ride in the booster seat in the back of your parents' car. . . . Almost every day something happens that will never happen again, without our knowing. Usually, these things aren't a huge deal, but when you look back, you might wish you had appreciated that time a little more.

The last Christmas with my Grammie and Grandpa was different. Even though no one really knew it would be the last, it had a feeling of special importance that everyone appreciated. The day was magical. The warm glow of the Christmas tree seemed to also live somewhere inside me. We had already opened our presents at our house that morning, but my sisters and I had the excitement of Grammie and Grandpa's gift ahead of us. We sat in the living room—my family, both my uncles and their wives, my three cousins, and Grammie and Grandpa. Even though Grandpa was very thin and weak, it seemed like everyone's worries were on hold, as even he was able to sit in his chair next to the tree while we all opened our gifts. I almost fell out of my seat when I unwrapped the deluxe Barbie mall I had given up hope on getting.

My Grammie had the most beautiful drinking glasses that had been passed down to her from her relatives in Italy. Some were blue and some were red, and they were hand-painted with little flowers and dipped in real gold. She only used them on Christmas. While everyone admired them, I think I loved them the most. Because they were so delicate, the young children did not get to use them. This Christmas, though, after we opened gifts, Grammie called me into the kitchen. I watched as she poured sparkling grape juice into one of the beautiful blue cups and handed it to me as we all made our way to the dining table.

Just when I thought there was no more room in my stomach, Grammie would bring out another big plate of food. It was hard work trying to save space for the many desserts that would follow, but I somehow managed. Everyone was in a festive mood, laughing and joking and telling stories about when my dad and his brothers were young. When we left to go see my Mimi and Pop-Pop later in the day, I felt so grateful for having such a big, wonderful family.

The week after Christmas is the one time my parents let the house stay messy with our toys. Usually, they are on us about keeping things tidy and put away where they belong. But, for this one week, all our new toys we got as presents can be scattered all over the living room. I spent that week playing and putting the finishing touches on the next issue of the *Orange Street News*.

Still thinking about how dangerous some of my neighbors seemed to think our town was, I decided to interview a Selinsgrove police officer to get the real story. (Spoiler alert: it was really safe!) I also decided to begin including a short fiction story that I wrote in each issue. I had so much fun making up a tale of haunted dolls in an attic. My "Message from Hilde" was about New Year's resolutions. Mine were morning bike rides on the weekends, creating new holidays, and watching my baby sister, Juliet, grow and play (maybe I wasn't such a jerk after all!). When it was time to return to school on Monday, January 5, I felt like I'd had the best Christmas break of my life.

When I got home from school, my mom had just gotten back from coffee with my Grammie. Again, my parents greeted me with enthusiasm, but I could tell something was off. I had my snack and decided to go up to my bedroom.

On my way up the stairs, I overheard my parents talking. "I mean, she's under so much stress, Matt. They need to get some answers. Clearly, something is wrong with him," my mom said.

"You know my mom is always stressing about something. She'll be all right. Once they get the results of the scan tomorrow, we can figure out what to do. I think she'll feel better when they have a plan," my dad responded.

"I hope so. She was just so upset today, Matt. I mean she really didn't seem good at all."

The next day when I left for school, I knew that my Grammie would be taking my Grandpa to have a PET scan. This is a type of test where they inject dye into a person and then basically take pictures of the tissues and organs to see how they are functioning. My Grandpa was having this test to see if his cancer was back. Everyone was really nervous, hoping for the best while preparing for the worst.

When I came home from school that day, my mom was rushing around frantically, trying to get baby Juliet changed and into her car seat.

"What's going on?" I asked.

"Grammie's been in an accident, Hilds. Dad and Izzy are already there, but we need to hurry. She's at the hospital. I don't know any more than that. Dad's trying to find out what's going on now."

20

THE SADDEST TUESDAY

I T WAS TUESDAY, but my dad and Izzy had gone to Grammie and Grandpa's earlier in the day to take down the Christmas tree. At some point, my uncle Andy called my dad to say Grammie had been in a car accident in the parking lot of the hospital. My dad left Izzy at the house and rushed to the hospital, only a mile away. As I rode in the car with my little sisters to Grammie and Grandpa's house, I tried to comfort myself by thinking that an accident in a parking lot couldn't be that bad.

But in the initial moments afterward, there was much confusion and the information we were getting turned out to be inaccurate. When we got to my grandparents' house, my dad's car was in the driveway. I let out a big sigh of relief. If Grammie was in really bad shape, my dad would have been at the hospital. As soon as we parked, I noticed my Mimi's car was there too. I thought that was strange. Usually, my Mimi and Pop-Pop only came to Grammie and Grandpa's house for big occasions like birthdays or holidays. I watched as my mom ran to my Mimi's car. In what seemed like only seconds, Mom sprinted as fast as she could into the house. My Mimi came to us, still in the backseat of my mom's car. She looked like she had been crying. The sinking feeling in my stomach returned.

"Where's Grammie? Is she OK?" I asked, my voice sounding more frantic than I wanted it to.

"Let's get your sisters out," was all she said in response.

As Mimi set about unbuckling Juliet from her car seat, I reached over and set Georgie free from her booster. I felt sick and confused and worried—so, so worried. Even though it felt like hours passed, my mom came back out in what was just a few minutes. She gave Mimi a hug, thanked her, and began leading us inside.

My dad was standing inside the entry to my grandparents' house. Something didn't look right about him, but I couldn't place what it was.

"Come with me, Hilds," he said as he started walking up the stairs to the room we used to sleep in when we would visit from Brooklyn. My mom stayed downstairs with my little sisters. I didn't know where Izzy was.

My dad began speaking, but I couldn't make sense of the words he was saying. My mind had latched on to one sentence and kept replaying the words over and over in a broken loop: *Grammie died.*

What really happened (the short version): Grammie died of a broken heart.

What really happened (the longer story): My Grammie took my Grandpa to have his PET scan. Because Grandpa was so weak, she didn't want him to have to walk to the parking lot afterward, so she went to pull the car around for him. The doctors told us that almost immediately after she started the car, her heart stopped. She must have had her foot on the gas pedal because as she went unconscious, her car smashed into the parking barrier.

There was a lot of discussion about why Grammie's heart stopped. The doctors talked about her high blood pressure and the fact that she was overweight. "Was she under any stress?" they asked my dad.

Of course we all knew that Grammie's heart couldn't handle the idea of losing Grandpa.

Two days later, the day before my Grammie's funeral, we got the results of my Grandpa's PET scan: the cancer was back and it had spread all throughout his body. All of Grammie's worries came true. Just five short weeks after my Grammie passed away, my Grandpa died from his cancer.

Hilde's Grammie and Grandpa, Gina and Arthur Lysiak.

21

THE AFTERMATH

⎯⎯⎯⎯⎯⎯

STARTED WETTING the bed.

This is not something I have ever told anyone outside of my family. But I cannot describe what I felt like during those first few months after my grandparents' deaths without including it. There was nothing medically wrong with me. Sometimes we forget that our bodies are very connected to our emotions. Bed-wetting was my reminder. In my case, the sadness and emptiness I felt over losing my grandparents caused my body to go a little crazy for a while. Doctors say this can happen after a child goes through a trauma. Losing my grandparents so suddenly and unexpectedly was traumatic to my whole family. We all just handled it differently.

My dad stopped eating. Because he is such a strong and upbeat person, he tried very hard not to show us how upset he was. He talked with me and my sisters about how we were feeling every day to make sure we were OK. But even though he was putting on a happy face, we saw that he was losing weight and knew how sad he really was too.

My mom was more expressive. She cried a lot in the days and weeks afterward. She didn't try to hide it from us because she thinks it's good to be sad when something bad happens.

Izzy didn't talk about it much. Instead, she spent more and more time in her bedroom writing songs and playing guitar.

Juliet, of course, was only two months old, but Georgie, at three, was the most devastating to watch. Not only had she been very close with Grammie, but she was also too young to really understand what death was. This meant she would ask things like, "When Grammie comes back from the cemetery, will she look the same?" Then my mom would have to explain that Grammie wouldn't be coming back, and Georgie would cry and cry. Watching that made me feel even worse.

I didn't talk to anyone about how I was feeling. Looking back, I think that is why I started wetting the bed. Those sad feelings had to find a way out of my body somehow. At the time, of course, I didn't really understand that. All I knew was that I was an eight-year-old who had to start wearing Pull-Ups at night. So embarrassing! I remember getting invited to a sleepover birthday party for one of the girls from my class. I wanted to go but was too afraid that someone would find out. I remember talking with my mom about it and her hiding the Pull-Up inside a special section of my overnight bag where no one would see.

Even though I felt horrible, I had to fulfill the promise I had made to my Grammie to keep putting out the *Orange Street News*. She may have been gone, but she had bought all those subscriptions for our family and her friends. She didn't just invest in the paper, she invested in me. Plus, after the second issue of the *OSN* came out, I had two or three other subscribers in town.

At first, I had no ideas. I just stared blankly at my notebook, feeling almost as overwhelmed as when I first started. How was I ever going to do this?

One morning I was sitting in our backyard swinging on one of the swings. This is something I still do to this day to relax. Even though we no longer have a swing set, I walk to a playground where I can swing for hours if I need to really clear my mind. On this particular day, I was feeling low and very unmotivated, when I overheard my dad talking to our next-door neighbor, Pam.

"Yeah, Tori has actually raised almost $700. I can't believe it!" Pam said.

After Pam went back in the house, I went to ask my dad what they were talking about. As it turned out, Pam's daughter, Tori, was born very prematurely. She spent the first several weeks of her life in the hospital. So as Tori was about to turn eleven, she decided to ask for donations to the neonatal intensive care unit of the hospital where she was born. Pam thought it was a great idea, but no one thought she would be able to raise so much money.

Later that afternoon, I interviewed Tori and sent Izzy, who had taken over the role of photographer for the *OSN*, to take her picture. As I sat typing in my dad's office, I caught myself feeling happy. This was the first time I would realize that working at something you love can be a great escape from sadness. It also made me realize how expressing myself through writing felt a lot easier than talking.

Unfortunately, not all my escapes were so healthy. For as long as I can remember, I have loved sweets. There is probably not much science to support the existence of a sweet treat gene, but looking at my family, one definitely has to wonder. My Grammie struggled most of her life with her relationship to food. She loved eating more than anyone I had ever met, and desserts were her favorite. The problem was, she couldn't really stop herself from eating too much. Sadly, because of this, she became overweight and had health problems like very high blood pressure. Even though we all suspect Grammie ultimately died from sadness and worry, these underlying problems definitely didn't help. My dad loved sweets almost as much as Grammie. He learned early on, however, that if he was going to eat like that, he would have to be very active. For almost ten years, my dad has run five miles every single morning, without missing one day. As a result, he stays fit even though he eats way too many doughnuts.

In the months following Grammie's and Grandpa's deaths, I began eating a lot. I found myself always wanting something sweet. If I couldn't have that, I wanted bread or pasta. Food felt like something to look forward to—a little bright spot in a day of blah. This would be the beginning of years of struggle: my struggle with food, my health-obsessed mom's struggle with my eating, the struggle between my sweet-treat-eating dad and my mom's no-sugar policy.

At this point, I wasn't yet aware of how sugar affected my mood—I just knew I wasn't feeling well at all. When I ate these kinds of foods, I didn't just eat a little. It felt like there was a big hole inside me that I was trying to fill with food, but I never really could. The hole was always there. After I ate this way, I would feel really happy for an hour or so, but then I would feel horrible. It wasn't that my stomach would hurt (although sometimes it would)—it was that I would feel this horrible combination of anger and sadness. I started yelling and crying more. Any little thing my sisters did made me feel irate. Even something like my parents asking me to clean my room could set me off.

My mom, who is a big believer in food as medicine, immediately made the connection between what I was eating and the outbursts I was having. She knew I had good reason to be feeling sad, but she also recognized that the way I was handling it was making me feel worse. Her solution was to make sure that I always ate only whole foods—nothing processed—and no sugar. This, of course, made me miserable. All my friends ate crappy food, especially Kristen. It was super difficult to be around this and not be able to eat those things too.

School was the worst. It seemed like every week someone was having a birthday party with cupcakes the parents sent in. My mom sent the teacher a box of granola bars for me (and not even the good ones) that I could eat instead. Beyond it being terrible to watch everyone eat cupcakes while I couldn't, it was totally embarrassing. It made me feel like something was wrong with me. After expressing this to my mom, she eventually came up with a "compromise": a once-a-week sweet day. We did this for years. One day a week, I could pick anything I wanted and enjoy it. Really, it did little to make me feel better.

My mom and I have talked many times about how she handled my food issues. Looking back, I know she was right about how the food was affecting me. But we both agree that her taking control of my eating in the way she did only made things worse for me. It also added a new list of descriptors:

- Sugar sensitive
- Blood sugar issues
- Picky eater
- Emotionally reactive

It may seem as if I was a total mess during this time, but that is not exactly true. I have found from years of reporting and being around people at their very worst moments that even in the darkest times, people can still feel moments of joy. And I did. I had moments of great happiness. I still played with Kristen, I still enjoyed school for the most part, and more than anything, I really began to fall in love with my newspaper.

The third issue of the *OSN* came out the week before my Grandpa died. It did not contain as many stories as the month before, but I was proud that, considering the circumstances, I was able to put it out at all. The Tori story was the cover of the paper. Inside I included another short fiction story, this time something less scary (my life was feeling dark enough). There was a story about a seed exchange the town library was holding, and a new feature called "Word on the Street," in which I asked several people to give a short opinion on a local issue. Izzy came along with me to take the pictures.

The hardest part of that issue was my "Message from Hilde." I didn't know what I should write. In my very first issue, I introduced myself to the readers. The second issue came out on New Year's Day, so that was an obvious thing to discuss. As I sat in front of my blank screen, I was at a total loss for what to do.

Just then, my dad walked in. "What's up, Hilds? How's it coming along?" he asked.

"Not good," I said. "I'm stuck. I don't know what to write for my message."

"Don't overthink it, kiddo," he said. "Write what you know."

What I knew ("Message from Hilde," issue 3, February 2015):

Dear Readers,

On Tuesday, January 6th, I lost my gramma.

She had a heart attack and died. It made me sad. It made me mad.

My favorite memory of her was at her birthday. We had a surprise birthday party for her at my house a few weeks ago. She was opening her presents. I got her a deck of cards because we loved to play rummy together.

I think she is in a happy place watching me.

I really miss her and think about her all the time.

22

CARRYING ON

E VEN THOUGH IT WAS WINTER, I found that I wanted to be outside more and
more. I began walking to the Kind Cafe almost every morning. The
girls who worked there had taken a liking to me. They told me they
thought it was awesome that I could come in all by myself at eight
years old. I've never understood what the big deal was. I think almost
every other eight-year-old would have been able to do what I did if
their parents let them. The problem was, in Selinsgrove, it seemed
most of the parents didn't let their kids have even half of the freedom
our parents gave us. There were positives and negatives to this.

One of the best things about it was that I got a lot of attention.
Soon, when I came into the Kind Cafe in the morning, I was being
approached by strangers asking if I was the "little girl with the newspaper." These people seemed really impressed with what I was doing.
Because of this, they started giving me tips. This is when I really began
feeling like a true reporter. I think because there was no other newspaper dedicated only to the town of Selinsgrove, the townspeople were
happy to be able to have a place to voice their concerns. Some of the
tips they gave me, especially in the beginning, were not necessarily

the most exciting—lost pets, community events, stories of their loved ones who had accomplished things like running in a race—but they were great practice for me. They often involved interviewing more than one person, sometimes even a town official. I learned how to have really great manners when speaking to the local police and politicians. Soon, I added the town office to my list of places to stop by. Nancy, the secretary there, was so kind and helpful. I'd ask her if there was any news, and over time she began to give me some.

Getting attention could also be one of the worst things about my newspaper. I would find out that there were many other people like the ones I encountered passing out my paper that first day on Orange Street—people who thought I was doing something wrong by reporting, or people who thought my parents were irresponsible for letting me do it. But I was not the only kid in my family to face this. Izzy was about to realize how crazy people can be when they think a kid shouldn't be out and about by herself.

It was April and in Pennsylvania that means it's usually still chilly and rainy. Izzy was begging my mom to take her shopping at the mall. My mom didn't really feel like going in—as I recall, she may have even had baby spit-up on her shirt as they walked out the door—but said she'd wait in the car for twenty minutes so Izzy could go look around in the makeup department. Twenty minutes came and went, but there was no Izzy.

My mom was annoyed. Izzy has never really been great at being on time, so my mom figured she would have to call and remind her. But the call went unanswered. When it was going on a half hour, my mom started to worry. Izzy was never *that late* when my parents were waiting. My mom was about to get out of the car when she saw Izzy was calling.

"Mom!" Izzy yelled through tears. "This woman had a hold of me and wouldn't let me go!"

As my mom began sprinting toward the entrance to the department store, fearing the worst, Izzy explained she was now with a security guard. My mom's heart began to calm a little as she asked Izzy what happened. As it turned out, Izzy was looking around the makeup counter as planned when a woman who worked there began asking her where her parents were. When Izzy said she was by herself, the woman asked how old she was. The woman then informed Izzy that "eleven-year-olds are not allowed to be in the store alone" and proceeded to grab Izzy's arm and force her into one of the makeup chairs. Izzy, definitely not someone to mess with, began yelling and making a fuss. That is when the security guard came.

The security guard met my mom at the door with a distraught and very angry-looking Izzy next to her. My mom told me later that the security guard seemed to think the makeup counter worker overreacted but thought my mom would just shrug it off and take Izzy home.

How wrong she was. My mom, in her shirt covered in baby spit-up, was a force of nature. Within minutes, while Izzy waited in the car, she was meeting with the head of department store security. The explanation that was given (and this would become a running theme over my years of reporting alone) was that the counter woman was "concerned for Izzy's safety." There seems to be some disconnect between what these people think and how they behave. The truth is the only thing that put Izzy in danger that day was the woman trying to "protect" her.

I've had strangers follow me trying to get me to get into their cars because they didn't think I should be walking the two blocks to school alone, I've had people call the police because I was out reporting by myself (as if that were a crime), and countless other people have begun message threads on social media about my "negligent" parents. Luckily my parents never let this bother them.

Not only did my mom get a formal apology from the department store owner that day, but management also clarified with its employees that there is absolutely no such policy that prevents eleven-year-olds (or any child, for that matter) from shopping alone in the store.

What was even better than the apology was that I had a great cover story for the May 2015 issue of the *Orange Street News*.

23

SCHOOL'S OUT (FOR GOOD)

W HILE MY FAMILY WAS STILL RECOVERING from the shock of losing Grammie and Grandpa, reporting became an outlet of happiness for us all. I was out every single day, sometimes interviewing people, sometimes poking around for stories, sometimes passing out my paper. I checked my e-mail several times a day, as I would get a few tips a week that way.

My number of subscribers had grown tremendously. By the time the school year was over, I had at least fifty people who had paid to get a copy of the *OSN* once a month for an entire year. Because I had more work, Izzy was also much busier. Not only was she taking photos for the paper, but I also began to incorporate video interviews. This was made possible by the fact that Izzy helped me set up a web page for the *Orange Street News*.

My dad continued working on his new book. Slowly, he began getting his bounce back in his step even though he still didn't seem like himself. My mom was busy with running the house and having a

The Lysiak family, three months after the death of Hilde's Grammie and Grandpa, take a much-needed break in Charleston, South Carolina.

baby and a three-year-old. She didn't cry as much as when my grandparents first died, but she also didn't seem to be back to her happy self.

So when my dad got a call from the *New York Daily News* wanting to send him on a big breaking news story in Charleston, South Carolina, it seemed like the perfect distraction for us all. Even though my dad had officially quit the paper, he was still able to work freelance for them. Many reporters and news photographers work on a freelance basis, which means they work for many different news outlets on a job-by-job basis. Since my dad was still considered one of their best reporters, the *New York Daily News* would still call him and ask him to work when a really big story broke. If he wasn't too busy with writing his book at the time, and, more important, if the rest of the family was all right with it, he went. It was in his blood.

Even though it was spring, it was rainy and chilly in Selinsgrove when we drove off toward Charleston. We left in the dark—my dad's favorite time to drive. As the miles passed and the light began to grow, there was a noticeable shift in the mood of the car. It seemed like the farther we got from Pennsylvania, the lighter we all felt. Even though we couldn't permanently separate from it, it was a relief to leave so much grief behind.

My dad was sent to cover the Walter Scott shooting. Much like the story that had sent us to Florida for a month my kindergarten year, race was at the center of this story. This time, however, the shooter was a police officer. Video footage showed Walter Scott, who had been stopped for having a broken brake light on his car, running from the police officer as the officer shot him eight times in the back. Scott was unarmed. Michael Slager, the police officer, pled guilty to second-degree murder and obstruction of justice and was sentenced to twenty years in prison.

Aside from the racial implications of the story, it also showed the importance of citizen journalism—not an unrelated issue. This would come to have so much relevance in my life. But, at this point, it was the first time I understood that this type of journalism—reporting or photography that is done by people who are not professional journalists but who put out information using websites, blogs, and social media—has the power to change lives.

In the case of Walter Scott, the police officer lied. He said that Scott was armed and that he had to shoot him in order to protect his own life. What Slager did not realize was that there was someone watching the incident—someone with a cell phone, a cell phone with a video camera. This citizen filmed the event and was able to make public what happened, contributing arguably the most serious piece of evidence against Slager.

As my dad shared all the details of the story with us, I felt lit up inside. I was, of course, outraged at what had happened. But beyond that, I felt a powerful excitement. I did not need to work for a fancy grown-up newspaper. I had a cell phone and the Internet at home. It was the first time I felt—I *knew*—I could make real change as a reporter in the world.

Because there was so much to cover about the Walter Scott shooting, our trip to Charleston lasted more than a week. When my dad first got the call to go, we had little notice and my mom was not able to call the school beforehand to arrange for my absence. When she did call them, we were already far out of Pennsylvania, unable to turn back (not that we would have).

An hour or so later, my mom got a call from the principal, who said he was upset about me missing school "again." I had missed a week when Grammie died, and then another week a month later when Grandpa died. I had also missed a few days in the beginning of the year to stay home and work on my paper. Since my dad was mostly working on writing books, he figured I could miss school here and there for reporting, just like I used to when I would go with him. It turned out the Selinsgrove elementary school was not as flexible as my little Lutheran school in Brooklyn had been.

My mom tried to very nicely explain to the principal that I had lost two grandparents in one month and that what was best for me was a break. She also mailed in documentation of the educational value of the trip. However, the school rules were that you had to give ten days' notice for a trip to be excused for educational purposes. Despite the fact that my mom explained that breaking news does not give notice, my absences were considered "illegal."

When we returned home, there was a letter waiting for us from the school. It said that if I missed any more days, my parents would be fined and could be reported to some government agency (none of us remember which agency exactly) for educational neglect. The letter was clearly a standard form they sent out to anyone who missed more than a certain number of days. There was little room for circumstances to be considered.

My mom was in the school office before we had unpacked our bags. The principal, while very nice, kept saying things like, "If I make an exception for your child, I'd have to make an exception for all of them." My mom was like, "For all the other children who are missing school to go help report on the biggest news story in the country?"

At the end of the day, my mom explained it to me like this: "Hilds, it's like we've been sitting on a fence with one leg on each side. On one side is the school and all their rules. On the other is the freedom we like to give you to have educational experiences you can't find in a classroom. It's like someone is taking down the fence and we need to pick a side. We're picking freedom."

And so I became a homeschooler again.

24

HOME AGAIN

BECAUSE THERE WAS LITTLE MORE than a month between the Charleston trip and the end of the school year, my parents decided not to do any formal homeschooling with me. Since all I really wanted to do was go out reporting, they figured I was getting enough "real life" education. And it was true. Working on the *OSN* involved public speaking, reading, writing, critical thinking, civics, and even some business math.

The weather had finally warmed in Selinsgrove. Everywhere was green and full of flowers. We all began to get used to Grammie and Grandpa being gone. That sounds terrible to say, but it's true. Of course, we missed them very much and still had moments of great sadness, but we also saw that life could move on, that happiness could still exist. I finally adjusted to baby Juliet, now six months old. And I stopped wetting the bed. As much as the first half of being eight was really crappy, the second half began to feel really good.

When it came time for kids to return to school, I remained home. A typical day for me began with coming down for breakfast with my family. Afterward, my mom would work with me for an hour or so on math, history, or science. My English education was fulfilled through my work on the *OSN* and afternoon reading. When "school" was over, I'd rush upstairs to get dressed and grab my tote bag with my notebook and pens. I also had a cell phone at this point since I was out and about by myself a lot. It came in handy, too, if Izzy wasn't around and I needed to get a picture of something or someone I was writing about. If I didn't have an interview scheduled, I'd head to the Kind Cafe, get a nice hot drink, and chat with the regulars. Most days I left with at least one story idea.

And the stories were getting more and more serious. At this point, I had covered important events, like a church fire, a home break-in, a tornado, and a bear on the loose in town. By the time my sixth issue came out, I had almost one hundred subscribers and at least ten people who regularly e-mailed me news tips.

I enjoyed the hustle and bustle of my life so much. It seemed like every day there was something I could set out to accomplish. I began to make lists for myself in the morning. It felt so amazing at night to look at all the items I was able to cross off.

Every now and then I felt I needed some downtime. When I wanted a little break, usually after an issue of the *OSN* came out, my parents would drive me to my Mimi and Pop-Pop's house an hour away. Sometimes I would stay the night; sometimes I'd stay a week. My Mimi worked at a law office full time, so it would be just me and Pop-Pop during the day.

Pop-Pop was my mom's grandfather, so he was my great-grandfather. He was honestly the sweetest, most joyful man I have ever known. At this point, he was in his nineties and pretty forgetful. He loved to look through old photos of his wife, my Mammy, who had died several years earlier, and tell me all about when his plane was shot down in World War II. He often didn't remember that he had already told me certain stories, so he would repeat them. I loved this. I got to know the stories so well I felt like I had lived them myself. It also reinforced the importance of writing things down. Memories fade. If we do not record them, history is lost.

But what happens when a person doesn't want a memory to last? I was about to find out.

25

MEET THE PLANT VANDAL

_____

A S I WAS ABOUT TO TURN NINE, I began getting tons of calls and e-mails about plants being torn up in town. Even though the downtown of Selinsgrove was small, it was well maintained with a square in the center known as the Commons. This is where the Saturday farmers market was held, where bands played on Thursday nights, and where the giant Christmas tree lighting took place. A nonprofit community organization known as SPI (Selinsgrove Projects Inc.) landscaped the Commons with an array of beautiful plants, flowers, and trees. In addition, many business owners on the main street planted flowers outside their shops.

On October 18, 2015, I started getting a slew of messages saying that sometime during the night, someone came through and ripped out the landscaping. Even though one business had a surveillance camera able to capture a partial image of the plant vandal, more than two months later, no arrest had been made, and the vandalism continued. Here is my "Message from Hilde" from December 29, 2015:

Dear Readers,

On January 1st it will be 68 days since the Selinsgrove Police had footage of the plant vandal and still they haven't found him.

68 days!!!!

The vandals in Selinsgrove are now doing more than ripping up flowers. In December they stole a red wagon right off someone's porch.

Luckily, the wagon was recovered, but if something isn't done to stop this vandalism I think it is only going to get worse.

My New Year's resolution is going to stay on the trail of the bandit until he or she is finally brought to justice.

Thank you for reading this issue of the Orange Street News and Happy New Year!

Sincerely,

Hilde Kate Lysiak

Publisher

Orange Street News

Between October 2015 and April 2, 2016, I wrote over twenty stories about the plant vandal. Because my subscriber count kept growing, I even had enough money to begin offering a cash reward of one hundred dollars for information leading to the arrest of the vandal. When no one came forward, I doubled the reward. Still nothing.

Then finally, at 2:00 AM on April 2, police witnessed the vandal in action and made an arrest:

BREAKING: VANDAL ARRESTED!!

April 2, 2016

By Hilde Kate Lysiak

Selinsgrove Police caught their man!

The menacing plant vandal that has been terrorizing Selinsgrove for months may have finally been stopped!

Selinsgrove Chief of Police Thomas Garlock told the
Orange Street News that law enforcement witnessed the
vandal tearing up the plants 2 am in the morning.

Police wouldn't reveal his name or age, but said it was
a man.

Police also wouldn't say if the vandal was connected to
the rash of Selinsgrove crimes.

The man would face a $200 to $300 fine, according to
Garlock.

THIS IS BREAKING STORY: CHECK BACK FOR
UPDATES!

I had my work cut out for me. After pursuing the vandal for
six months, I couldn't wait to get an interview with him. It was going
to be difficult enough to get the vandal to agree to speak with me, but
before I could even set out on that task, I had to first get his name.
This meant many hours of waiting outside the Selinsgrove Police
Department.

Most of the officers in town were nice to me. One or two were
not. But even the nicer police officers were sometimes reluctant to
give me information. I had a feeling it wasn't going to be easy to get
the vandal's name, but I did not think that it would take ten days!
Day after day, I would show up outside the police station and ring the
bell. Sometimes no one would answer. Sometimes they would tell me
they didn't know (which was highly suspicious). After the receptionist
told me that the police were "too busy driving around the school" to
talk to me, I had had enough. When the government (in this case, the
local police) makes an arrest, it is not their information to keep. The
public has a right to know the suspect's name. If the police weren't
going release it, I felt it was the job of the *OSN* to demand it.

I remembered the power of video, and on day nine, Izzy filmed
me recording a special report from outside the police station. In it, I

ORANGE STREET NEWS INVESTIGATION

Hilde, nine, reporting from the Selinsgrove Police Department as she tries (again) to get the name of the plant vandal.

told the viewers that it had been nine days since the vandal's arrest and still the police had not released the name to the public. Izzy filmed me ringing the bell to the station and waiting. No one answered. We biked home and immediately put it up online. It definitely did not reflect positively on the police department. What if I had been in trouble? Ignoring someone ringing the bell to the police station seemed negligent.

The police must have realized this too, because the very next morning, they released the name of the plant vandal. It turned out he was a twenty-one-year-old student about to graduate from the local college. Within an hour of googling, I was able to get his contact information. When he never responded, I wrote my story without an interview.

I'm not sure if he even knew what the *Orange Street News* was at that point. But in just a few days, the whole world would find out. And as a young person applying for his first professional job, having his name in my paper would prove to be quite a problem for the plant vandal.

26

EXCLUSIVE: MURDER ON NINTH STREET

————

I WAS BEYOND SICK of the plant vandal and I was feeling pretty over the Selinsgrove Police Department too. So when the town Chocolate Stroll approached, I found myself unusually excited to cover it.

The Chocolate Stroll was the idea of one of my favorite *OSN* subscribers. Helen Walter was the owner of the Cottage on Pine, an antiques business, and the president of the town's Chamber of Commerce. She was also the first business to pay to advertise in the *Orange Street News*. Helen was very creative and worked tirelessly to get more people to shop in the downtown area. This most recent event involved trying to get people into the stores by promising them free chocolate treats.

By this point—almost a year and a half after starting the *OSN*—I normally disliked covering events. But a newspaper is like a soup—the ingredients must be balanced or the soup won't taste good. If all I ever reported on was heavy stories like vandalism and fires, my subscribers might stop reading. Even though lighthearted community events were not very exciting for me to cover, I found my readers did want that information. Today, I was happy to give it to them. Little did I know my entire life was about to change in a few short hours.

My work for the day involved going to each participating business, with Kristen at my side, sampling whatever yummy chocolate treat they made and interviewing business owners to find out if the Chocolate Stroll was increasing business as intended. I felt happy and light (and maybe a little hopped up on sugar) and grateful to have this rare moment when my best friend could be part of my reporting.

When I look back, I think of the strangeness of my last real kid moment: Kristen and I standing inside a little shop that sold yarn and candles. It was warm, and the scents of lavender and vanilla filled the air. By the counter, a large platter held chocolate eggs laid out in all their deliciousness. They looked like the peanut butter eggs my grandmother's church made around Eastertime. They were my favorite. Kristen and I each happily grabbed one and crammed them into our mouths, only to realize they were real eggs. We were eating chocolate-covered hard-boiled eggs! I have hated eggs my entire life. I find them to be one of the grossest things around. Kristen and I looked at each other, eyes wide, and kept chewing. There was something strangely yummy about these eggs.

As we left the store, we were laughing like crazy. It was one of those moments in time when everything felt glowy and clear. I couldn't find a trace of sadness anywhere inside my body. Everything felt light and joyous. I was with my best friend, doing something I loved. It couldn't get any better. And then my phone pinged.

Over the six months that I had covered the plant vandal, I gained many supporters. Though there was no other newspaper that covered only Selinsgrove, the *Daily Item*, a newspaper in the next town over, covered Selinsgrove as well as several other towns. Apparently, someone vandalizing plants wasn't big enough news for them, because they gave the story no coverage despite the fact that many residents reached out to them. When those residents grew frustrated that their voices weren't being heard, they began, one by one, to contact me. I took them seriously and stayed on the story. Because of that, many townspeople became loyal to the *Orange Street News*.

When I checked the notification on my phone, I saw I had an e-mail from one of these supporters. Because the plant vandal had been arrested, I almost didn't read the e-mail right away—I couldn't imagine anything really time sensitive had happened. Oh, how wrong I was. The e-mail read something like this:

> Dear Hilde,
> I thought you should know, something terrible has happened. A man has murdered his wife. I don't have many details but thought you'd want to check it out.
> Thanks,
> [Name withheld for privacy]

I felt my face get very hot. My heart began to beat a million miles a second. I knew I had to move, and I had to move fast. But inside there was something other than excitement. There was fear. I looked at Kristen, who had chocolate smeared all over her face, and allowed myself a second to freak out. But if I had learned anything from reporting so far, it was that a reporter must always be ready. I searched through my mind for the basics. My racing heart began to calm. I knew what I had to do.

"I'll meet you back on Orange Street later on," I said to Kristen, who by now understood the look on my face.

"Get a good story," she said, having zero idea what had just happened.

I needed to find an address. I raced the two blocks on my bike to the police station. I found myself in the familiar yet annoying position of waiting behind an unanswered door. I clenched my fist and knocked again, this time with more urgency. Then waited.

Another knock. Nothing.

Again. I couldn't believe that here I was again, knowing something big had happened and feeling totally powerless to get the information I desperately needed.

I could feel my heart begin to race again. A reporter covering breaking news needs to be quick on her feet, especially when working a story that could be this important. If the tip was true, it could be the biggest story that had ever happened in Selinsgrove. That meant other reporters from the adult newspapers would soon be arriving on the scene. The *Daily Item* might not be interested in a plant vandal, but something told me they wouldn't miss the opportunity to cover a murder. I also knew from experience that witnesses are less likely to talk when they see a bunch of people around. If I got there first, I had a better chance of neighbors or witnesses opening up and sharing the truth.

I lifted my fist to pound the door and was about to strike again when it opened and a tall police officer emerged.

My heart sank. I remembered this guy. I had dealt with him before. He was never helpful. "Hi, I'm Hilde from the *Orange Street News* and I was wondering if you could—"

The officer interrupted. "I can't talk right now," he said.

In a whirl, he rushed past me and into his police car. My heart began to keep time with the screaming sirens as the police car raced out of the lot. I quickly shoved my notebook and pen in my bag, hopped on my bike, and gave chase.

Despite having rock-hard calf muscles from all the biking I did, I could not keep up with the speeding police car. I kept up until he turned off Pine Street. I kept pedaling as fast as I could, but when I rounded the corner, there was no trace of the officer. As I heard the sirens fade into the distance, I slowed by bike and took a minute to think.

I had tried calling my dad earlier, but he wasn't answering. I left him a message telling him what I knew. When I took my phone out of my pocket to see if I had missed his returned call, I noticed I had another e-mail from my source. My fingers shook as I opened it. Inside, in one simple sentence, I had my answer.

It read: "600 block of Ninth St." I was only a few blocks away!

At this point, in addition to the police, I was prepared to see several news trucks and reporters everywhere. Even though I had never covered a story this big on my own, I had been to several of these with my dad. But when I turned onto the block, I couldn't believe my eyes. Three police cars sat directly in front of the house. No one else.

Maybe my source was wrong? I caught myself feeling disappointed. There it was again: that weird disconnect between not wanting anything bad to have happened to anyone, yet wanting the "good" news story that comes from something bad happening. But I didn't really have much time to process this because all my instincts were screaming at me, telling me I needed to get to work. Three police cars meant *something* was going on.

Outside the house, I saw the grumpy police officer and a few other officers. There was one I recognized who had always been very kind and helpful to me. I decided to focus on him first.

"Excuse me, Officer. I'm Hilde Lysiak from the *Orange Street News*. I heard there was a murder here. Could you confirm that?"

"Sorry, Hilde, I cannot comment on anything that has happened here."

Then the grumpy officer came over and said, "You need to go home. This is no place for a kid."

Pushing it with the police never really amounted to anything other than annoying them, so I dropped it for the time being. But there was no way I was leaving. The grumpy officer basically just acknowledged that something had happened, or why else would it be "no place for a kid"? I knew from reporting with my dad that you can get the best information from people around the scene. I looked around at all the houses lining both sides of the street. I picked the home directly next door and began knocking.

A man answered at the first house. I couldn't even get through my introduction before he said, "I think you'd best go home, little girl."

I'll never understand what being a girl had to do with it. I mean, even though I didn't agree with people who thought I was too young to be a reporter, I at least understood their concern. But over and over again, my being a girl was a topic of conversation whose irrelevance baffled me. I let my irritation motivate me to move on.

There was no answer at the second house. I decided to cross the street.

Eventually, a woman answered one of the doors and wanted to talk. "Hi, Hilde. It's a very sad story, actually," she began. "The husband had a stroke a little while ago and hasn't been the same. From what I understand, he got very upset about something and killed his wife."

I kept my hand steady as I made sure to write down every single thing she told me exactly as she said it. There was no room for error in a story this big. I left her house and tried my dad again.

There were several things that were confusing me. First of all, I felt like I had a major exclusive. But I didn't know how much confirmation I needed before I could print the story. Was what one neighbor told me enough? I also didn't understand how it was possible that I was the only reporter on the scene if something as big as a murder happened. Still, my dad's phone went unanswered. I knew I could call my mom and she could track him down, but before I did that, I decided it would be a good idea to interview more neighbors.

Over the next half hour, at least three or four other neighbors told me the same thing: the husband in the home where the police cars were parked had murdered his wife. One reported seeing a body being removed from the home on a stretcher. Two different people also added that they heard the murder weapon was a hammer.

I looked around. It was one of the most surreal moments of my life. There I was, a nine-year-old kid, and the only reporter on the scene of what I had pretty well confirmed was a murder investigation. I even had a potential weapon. Where was everyone else?

A few of the neighbors gave me a clue that I would not realize until much later. Several of them told me, "They [the police] told us we can't talk about anything." Eventually, I would find out they had told all the news agencies the same thing. Is that why no one was around? Had the other papers and TV stations actually listened to the police when they said they didn't want them covering the investigation?

Probably the most important thing to understand about the press (meaning newspapers, online news, TV news, etc.) is that it must remain free. Not everyone agrees with me on this point, but I would tell you they are wrong. It is dangerous for the government to have any kind of control over the news. Remember, the police are part of the government. In our society, people need to know what is happening. They need the truth. If you don't have access to the truth, you can't live your life freely. If the government runs the news, what happens if the government is doing something wrong? The people would need to know that to be able to change it, right? Of course. But if the newspapers are all run by the government, they will never publish stories that will expose their own wrongdoing. That means the people can be easily taken advantage of, and their freedom completely lost.

So, standing on the 600 block of Ninth Street in Selinsgrove, Pennsylvania, I realized that the police not only were telling the people not to talk about what happened but had also told all the media that they couldn't either. What I didn't understand was, why would the media listen? As a publisher of a newspaper, I felt it was my responsibility to the people to tell them what happened. The police could try to turn me away, but there was no way I was going to listen. It was my legal right to be there asking questions, and I intended to do just that.

I headed back over to where the police were. I needed to run all the information I had gathered by them and see if they would confirm any of it. At this point, there were a few more people outside the house. I recognized one of them from some other stories I had worked on—the assistant district attorney. The state police had also arrived.

What was most noteworthy, however, was the white van parked out-side—the coroner. A coroner is an official who investigates violent, sudden, or suspicious deaths. This was another gigantic sign that all my sources were right—a murder had happened. Still, I needed official confirmation. I picked the friendliest-looking police officer, this time one of the state police, to approach.

"Hello, I'm Hilde Lysiak, publisher of the—"

"This is an ongoing investigation," he interrupted. "I'm going to have to ask you to leave."

"I have several sources telling me a man murdered his wife with a hammer inside this home. Can you please confirm this?"

The officer looked me in the eye while slowly nodding his head yes, then said, "This is an ongoing investigation."

Just then, my phone rang. It was my dad. "Oh my gosh—Hilds! I'm sorry, I went out for a drink, or actually a few drinks, and left my phone at home. Just heard your message. Do you know what's happening?"

"Uh . . . yeah, Dad. I've been here for almost an hour. I'm the only one besides the police and the coroner."

"The only one? Where's the other media?"

"The police are telling people not to talk. I guess they've even told the other news that they don't want them covering it. Why are they listening?"

"That's insane! Well, kiddo. This puts you in a fantastic position. What have you got so far?"

Over the next five minutes, I told my dad what I had and how I was confused if it was enough confirmation to run a story. He explained that it wasn't often that a reporter got official confirmation from the police. He said I most definitely had enough information to put up a story. I would just need to be careful about my wording and call the incident a "possible murder" or "suspected murder." The best part was I was going to have exclusive breaking coverage of the biggest story to happen in Selinsgrove in decades.

ORANGE STREET NEWS INVESTIGATION

Hilde, nine, first on the scene, reporting on the homicide.

My next call was to Izzy. I needed video. She arrived by bike five minutes later, opened her backpack up, and began recording.

I knew I was onto something big, but I had no idea the video Izzy and I were about to film would be viewed millions of times. I'd like to say that if I had known, I would have fixed my hair, but I probably wouldn't have. If you even look really closely, you can see faint chocolate smears on my face left over from the morning that now seemed a lifetime ago.

In the video, I'm standing across the street from the house where the murder took place. Police cars and yellow police tape are in the background. I do a quick, twenty-nine-second video (in which I talk for only nine seconds) where I give the basics: "Hi. Hilde Kate Lysiak here, reporting for the *Orange Street News*. I'm on the 600 block of Ninth Street where a man suspectedly murdered his wife with a hammer. I'm working hard on this ongoing investigation."

When Izzy was finished, she took my bike and raced home to get the video up online. From the scene, I began writing up my story. Within an hour of Izzy showing up, the video, along with this story, went public:

Exclusive: Murder on Ninth Street

By Hilde Kate Lysiak

Police are investigating a possible murder at 9th Street in Selinsgrove.

A man is suspected of murdering his wife with a hammer at 9th Street in Selinsgrove, sources told the Orange Street News.

"This is an ongoing investigation," an officer told the Orange Street News.

Residents reported seeing a person taken out on a stretcher but were told by police not to talk to media.

"They told us we can't talk about anything," one neighbor told the Orange Street News.

The woman is a former Selinsgrove borough employee. Many neighbors remembered her fondly.

"This is terrible. Just terrible," one neighbor told the OSN. "I can't believe this happened. She was such a wonderful woman. Very kind."

The suspected murderer was a retired schoolteacher at Selinsgrove and the victim also worked as branch manager at a local bank on Market Street, according to neighbors.

"They seemed like a good, loving couple," one neighbor told the Orange Street News. "I'm just in shock."

The Chief of police, District Attorney, PA State police, and Coroner are on the scene.

The Orange Street News is withholding the name of the victim to make sure friends and family are told first.

MUST CREDIT THE ORANGE STREET NEWS! THIS IS A BREAKING STORY. CHECK BACK FOR UPDATES

But my own news story was just beginning.

27

HATERS GONNA HATE

"**A**RE YOU KIDDING ME?!**" my mom yelled. "That is just unbelievable!" The combination of my super sleuth eavesdropping skills and my mom's near inability to hide her emotions led me to the living room. It was early morning, the day after the murder. I had stayed on the scene and managed to get the couple's names but had decided, on the advice of my dad, to withhold them in case not all family members had been notified of the woman's death.

Eventually, the other media began to show up, but by then I was hours ahead of them. By the time I made it home (before dark, per my parents' rule), my dad assured me no other media had anything more than I did. In fact, many were forced to credit me and my story because they were unable to get the information I had from any source besides the *Orange Street News*.

I was proud of my work. I did everything right. I stayed at the scene. I spoke to everyone on the block and got confirmation from law enforcement. Still, I had a hard time sleeping knowing that the adults could be on the scene later than I could. What if they got a great scoop while I was asleep? Was that what my mom was upset about?

I was planning on sitting at the top of the steps a while longer but then I heard my dad say: "He's the f—ing former mayor of the town! How can he justify publicly talking about a nine-year-old that way?!"

At that, I flew down the stairs. "What are you talking about? What's going on?" I asked.

My parents looked a little like the cat that ate the canary—a weird expression my Mammy used to use that basically means they were caught talking about something they didn't want anyone else to hear. I saw the heat rise in my mom's face as she looked at my dad. There was a long pause when I felt like they were working something out in a silent language. Finally, my dad spoke.

"Sit down, kiddo," he said.

I didn't want to sit down. Suddenly, I felt very awake. But I did what I was told and took the chair opposite where my parents were sitting on the couch.

"I'm not sure that we should be telling you this," my dad said, for probably the hundredth time in my life. This meant something crazy was coming. "A lot of people are talking about your coverage of the murder. It was the biggest story in the history of this small town and for several hours, Hilds, you were the only place the people of the town could get information."

"But?" I said, knowing there was more on the way.

"But a lot of people are really mad and saying some very mean things," my mom said.

"Whatever. There's always going to be people that don't like my paper. They don't have to read it," I said.

By now, I was used to this. People complained that my headlines were too flashy or that I used too many exclamation points. They didn't like some of my word choices. I would even get e-mails from time to time where someone would send an edited version of one of my stories back to me. Unless it seemed they were truly trying to be helpful, I had just learned to ignore them.

"Well, this is different, Hilds. This is a small town, and people are angry. A lot of people. And they are saying some very screwed-up things about you," my dad said.

Five minutes later, I found myself sandwiched between my parents, reading the comments on the *Orange Street News* Facebook page. This was something my dad managed. My parents thought that at nine, I should not be on social media. And as long as Izzy could post my stories for me, I had little desire to be on there either. My heart began to pound as I read:

- *This article, paper, whatever it is, is a complete joke. Horrible.*
- *I usually enjoy your stories, Hilde, but this . . . perhaps you are too young to understand the difference between respect/decency and sensationalism.*
- *Sensationalist trash . . .* [This was written by the former mayor of Selinsgrove, who also happened to live across the street from us.]
- *I am disgusted that this cute little girl thinks she is a real journalist. Whatever happened to tea parties?*
- *Nine-year-old girls should be playing with dolls not trying to be reporters.*
- *You are nine f—ing years old. Seriously, what the f— is wrong with you.*

I didn't understand. From the moment I arrived on the scene, there was something very confusing going on. Between my being the first and only media outlet to report on the murder for several hours and people being upset that I reported it at all, something just didn't add up. What was most confusing was that none of these people who were upset had an issue with my journalism. My article was very straightforward and contained only facts. I brought the people the information, the truth. How was I being disrespectful? What was sensationalist about saying what was true?

But what made me angry was that I was being judged for things I had no control over: my age and gender. I had almost gotten used to people thinking it was weird or wrong for me to be reporting because of my age, but now why the heck were they telling me I belonged at home playing with dolls? It seemed like people thought I had no right to say what was true simply because I was a girl. What if I were a nine-year-old boy? Would that have been OK? What if I was a twenty-five-year-old woman? Would I then be allowed to speak the truth? Now that I'm fourteen, I realize there is a big problem with women and girls—of any age—being treated as "less than" because of their gender. But when I was nine, this was a completely foreign idea to me. It felt hugely unfair, and it made me angry. Very, very angry.

After reading the comments, I had a really long discussion with my parents about how I wanted to handle it. At first, it was kind of surprising, because my mom, who seemed even more bothered than my dad, thought I should ignore the haters. My dad, who seemed less worked up, thought that I should fight back in some way.

I was torn. I saw my mom's point. It has always been so impor-tant to me to let my work stand on its own. And I was super proud of my story. Part of me wanted to just disregard the negative com-ments and keep reporting. If people didn't like it, they didn't have to read it. But whenever I considered doing that, something inside me didn't feel right. I thought about how I would feel if someone had said those things to Izzy or Kristen. Would I want them to just walk away? Keeping quiet seemed to give these people what they wanted. They wanted to silence me. Because I was young. Because I was a girl.

I decided my dad was right on this one—it was time to speak up. But this didn't feel like it belonged in my paper. The OSN was for news. Sure, I had my "Message from Hilde," but that somehow didn't feel like enough. Thanks to the Internet, it seemed like my video coverage was reaching even more people than my paper. I decided I wanted Izzy to film me talking directly to the haters.

I wrote down what I was feeling and told Izzy to hit record. This is what I said:

Hilde Kate Lysiak here, reporting from the *Orange Street News*. Yesterday, there was a murder in Selinsgrove. It happened just a few blocks from my house. I got the tip from a good source that I was able to confirm. Then I went straight to the scene and asked neighbors for more information. I worked very hard. Because of my work, I was able to inform the people that there was a terrible murder hours before my competition even got to the scene. In fact, some of these adult-run newspapers were reporting the wrong news, or no news at all. All the while, the *Orange Street News* was out covering the murder. I know this makes some of you uncomfortable, and I know some of you just want me to sit down and be quiet because I'm nine, but if you want me to stop covering news, then you get off your computer and do something about the news. There. Is that cute enough for you? I'm Hilde Kate Lysiak. Thanks for watching. Izzy, shut this off. I'm done.

When we got home, my mom, now having gotten on board with my choice to speak out, had a suggestion. She pulled up a few episodes of the "Mean Tweets" segment of *Jimmy Kimmel Live!*—something I had never seen before. On his late-night talk show, Kimmel features celebrities reading mean comments people write about them on Twitter. They are hilarious. It is also a great way to make the haters look foolish.

Immediately, I set about selecting the worst comments people had made about me. When I had them picked out, Izzy filmed me reading them in our library. When I rewatched the two videos together, I was super happy with the results. I think they illustrated exactly what I wanted: the haters weren't bothering me, and I would not be silenced.

Afterward, when Izzy went upstairs to upload the videos, I decided to check my e-mail. I was hoping for some new tips, but instead my inbox was full of nothing but angry messages. Even some of my sources were mad. It felt like a giant ball of hatred rolling down a hill, getting larger and larger, coming directly for me and my parents. The town that I loved had turned against me. It wasn't just the mayor; it was other town officials too. And worse than that, many people seemed to believe the lies about me.

That was when I realized what was actually at stake—a newspaper might be paper and ink, but its main ingredient is credibility. It is built on trust, and with so many people in a small town saying untrue things about me, I realized that if I didn't correct the record I was going to lose the respect I had worked so hard to earn—and the *Orange Street News*.

Izzy posted the video and we waited.

28

IN THE NEWS

———

Modern Day Nancy Drew First to Cover Homicide
9-Year-Old Crime Reporter Breaks Murder Stories
    with No Fear
Girl Reporter, 9, Breaks Murder Story
Journalist, 9, Responds to Her Critics and Becomes
    a Media Star
Child Reporter Inadvertently Distracts from Mur-
    der Case

THE REQUESTS BEGAN POURING into my e-mail almost immediately. After my dad posted my response videos, nearly every major news organization, be it television or print, was reaching out to interview me. Before the day was over, my videos had gone viral, and headlines were splashed all over the Internet.

To be fair, my dad was connected to many reporters and editors from his time as a journalist in New York City. So when he shared the videos on his own social media accounts, people from the *New*

York Times, New York Daily News, New York Post, CBS, NBC, etc. saw them. Having them reach out to me made the entire reporting situation come full circle. My dad's reporting was what inspired my own. Now, after I had spent years admiring him and his coworkers, it was my work that they wanted to cover. It felt amazing to be recognized by these journalists.

But it was also overwhelming. I am not the type of person who loves being the center of attention. Being a reporter, I could get out and talk with people (which I loved) without the story ever being about me. Now, everyone wanted to know what I was doing and what I thought. It made me slightly uncomfortable. Also, I hated how so much of the conversation centered on my age or my being a girl. Why was it so shocking that a nine-year-old girl could do something like be a reporter? Of course, the older I got, the more I realized that we do not live in a world where great things are expected of young girls. I certainly hope that my story has helped change even a little of that.

At first, I was uncertain if I wanted to be interviewed by anyone. On the one hand, I felt I had accomplished everything I set out to do by making my videos. On the other hand, television shows were offering to send personal drivers to scoop me and my family up and whisk us away to fancy hotels in New York City. I had been missing the hustle and bustle of New York so much. I thought about all the amazing food, all the great coffee shops and bakeries, and seeing my old friends in Brooklyn. I also thought it would be an excellent opportunity to get a behind-the-scenes look at how television media was run. *Who knows, maybe I would want to do that someday,* I thought.

The next week was a whirlwind of appearances. My mom and I were on *Good Morning America, The Real Story with Gretchen Carlson* on Fox News, and *Reliable Sources* on CNN. Everyone wanted to know how I felt about the sexist comments I received. When I look back on these interviews, it strikes me how simple my view of it was. "It annoyed me," was the answer I most used, still having little understanding that this was not an experience specific only to me. In my mind, these people who said I had no right to report because I was a girl were just jerks who were wrong. I now know that, unfortunately, this belief system is a slithery snake of an idea sliding through many of the societies around the world.

One of the opportunities that came from all my publicity was the chance to interview Malala Yousafzai. The sexism in her story was not just a slithery snake—it was an anaconda with lightning speed. Malala, who grew up in Pakistan, was shot because she insisted on going to school. Can you imagine not being able to get an education simply because you are a girl? Would you be willing to risk your life to secure that right? What I did in standing up to my critics was certainly not as brave as taking a bullet, like Malala did, but I believe with all my heart that exploding the silence is the first step toward changing this grotesque way of thinking. People who think girls shouldn't be able to do the same things as boys usually also hold a belief that girls are quiet and meek. My critics thought they would type out their terrible comments and I would be silent. I say smash that silence!

The media appearances ended up being overwhelmingly fun. After leaving my *Good Morning America* appearance, I was shocked to find photographers waiting for me outside. As flashes went off in every direction, with people shouting out, "There she is! There she is!" I looked over to see Izzy, who was usually unimpressed with me, beaming with pride. It felt good to be something other than her annoying little sister, if only for a few moments.

As the interviews faded, interesting opportunities kept coming my way. I was chosen by Target, along with nine other kids, to create our own line of clothing. Each one of us was picked for doing something special at a young age and flown to the Target headquarters in Minneapolis. There were dancers and photographers, inventors and entrepreneurs. We ranged in age from seven to fourteen. As my mom and I exited the hotel elevator that first morning, I felt super nervous and

Hilde, nine, about to interview one
of her greatest inspirations, Malala
Yousafzai.

insecure when I caught sight of all the flashy kids gathered together in
the lobby. They all seemed to have come with their own personal stylist.
I looked down at my striped knee socks and beat-up sneakers and swal-
lowed the lump that was forming in my throat. I tried to remind myself
that if I was there to interview them, I would feel excited, not nervous,
so I just pretended that's what I was doing until I got over my jitters.

The other kids were all very nice to me and I had fun getting to
know them. It just seemed that many of them were under so much
more pressure than I was. Some of them even had people filming their

experience at Target to post to social media accounts that had upward of a million followers. That level of fame was nothing I was interested in. If I could walk a line between being able to live a normal life and still getting these cool opportunities, I'd be happy.

As time went on, that seemed to be the case. I'd have my normal life of waking up, doing school with my mom, then going out reporting. Then, it seemed like every few weeks I'd get to go do something cool. One spring, Google even flew Izzy and me, along with our mom, to its campus to celebrate World Press Freedom Day. We got a personal tour of the campus, where we saw the self-driving cars and the amazingly cool nap pods the workers had for when they needed a break (sign me up!), and we even got to meet the team that designs the Google graphics. Of course, the thing that caught my attention the most was the impressively stocked kitchens in each office building. It was a paradise of yummy snacks and drinks. And of course, as nothing was off limits to us, I made good use of them.

One day, my dad, now an established book author, was approached by Scholastic about publishing a series of books based on my real-life reporting. They would be for their Branches line, which is aimed at kids just beginning to read chapter books on their own. Each one centered on an actual story I had published in the *Orange Street News* but was then fictionalized. Of course, I wasn't able to write them myself. In the beginning, my dad did most of the work while I just gave him ideas. But as the series went on—there ended up being six books in total—and I got older, I became more involved. By the time *Thief Strikes!*, the final book in the series, was published, I was typing out a good portion of the story myself.

Shortly after I broke the news of the homicide, Izzy and I were given a Disruptive Innovation Award from the Tribeca Film Festival. These awards "celebrate the awe, wonder, and enchantment of innovation, recognizing innovators disrupting the status quo for the public good." Basically, the award is for people who disrupt, or disturb, an existing system that is flawed but widely accepted—like sexism. Izzy and I were chosen for how we handled the haters. This was another opportunity to go to New York City. This time, though, we had to go onstage in front of hundreds of people to accept our award. Izzy and I worked hard preparing and memorizing our speeches. This was when I first fell in love with public speaking. Being in front of all those people and hearing them cheer for what I was saying was such a rush.

Little did we know that sitting two rows behind us was Joy Gorman Wettels, a big shot television producer responsible for shows such as *Thirteen Reasons Why*. Apparently, I wasn't the only one who felt the rush of my speech. Several weeks after the Disruptive Innovation Awards, we got a call from Joy. She wanted to make a television show based on my reporting! We reached an agreement with her and her production company, Anonymous Content, and the seeds of what would become the Apple TV+ show *Home Before Dark* were planted.

But speaking of plants, while we waited for the television show to be made, back in Selinsgrove an old friend was about to resurface.

29

RETURN OF THE PLANT VANDAL

AS I SETTLED BACK into my reporting life, an old friend came out of the woodwork: the plant vandal, who had ignored all my interview requests, suddenly was eager to talk with me. He began sending me e-mails asking to arrange a meeting. After six months of working so hard on that story, I was really bummed out that I never got the chance to interview the vandal. I had so many questions—the biggest of which was simply "What were you thinking?!" Of course I would meet with him! I wondered what had changed his mind.

And then I found out. The plant vandal was a recent college graduate who was applying for his first real job. Now that the *Orange Street News* had gotten so much press, when employers googled the vandal's name, the first thing that came up was my article about him being arrested in the little town of Selinsgrove for ripping up plants. Not exactly the type of person someone wants to hire. The vandal wanted to meet with me to convince me to remove his name from all my articles.

At first, I was mad. Of course I wouldn't remove his name. Wouldn't that basically be the same thing that I'd been criticizing the other local media for—picking and choosing stories according to people's feelings? Still, I wanted to meet this vandal so desperately. I decided to talk with my dad.

When I ran the situation by him, he asked me one very important question: "Would your readers benefit more by keeping his name online or hearing his story?"

"His story," I answered.

"There's your answer," my dad said, like some mystical monk, as he walked out of the room.

I sat there for a moment and then it hit me. I opened up my e-mail and began typing as fast as I could. I offered the vandal a deal that he couldn't resist: if he gave me a full interview all on the record, I would remove his name from all the articles.

Two days later, I sat with my tape recorder at a table in the Kind Cafe. He was ten minutes late. Just as I was starting to think he wouldn't show, in walked a very normal-looking young man. He looked like someone who would carry an old lady's groceries to her car—not the scary vandal I was expecting. As he took the chair opposite me, I noticed he was sweating a bit. He was nervous! I was really enjoying myself.

We sat for an hour. Not only did he answer all my questions and allow me to tape the interview, but he also insisted that he be able to apologize to the people of Selinsgrove. Here is the transcript of that interview:

> **OSN: How do you feel that you were caught?**
> VANDAL: You know, obviously, I feel bad for the people
> that own the plants. Obviously, you know, people try
> to decorate the town and they don't think that this
> can happen. I'm embarrassed that I let my anger get

the best of me that night and, ya know, I have to live
with the consequences.

OSN: **And so, are you sorry for vandalizing Selinsgrove?**

VANDAL: Yes, I am. I became friends not just [with] people
within the Susquehanna community but within Selinsgrove. I'm sorry that I did what I did.

OSN: **What were you thinking when you were ripping up
those plants?**

VANDAL: Well, see, I only ripped up one plant.

OSN: **Well, what were you thinking when you did it?**

VANDAL: When I ripped up the plant?

OSN: **Ah ha.**

VANDAL: I was angry and I saw an opportunity to take out
my anger and I shouldn't have. That's the story with
my thoughts there.

OSN: **Did you think you wouldn't be caught?**

VANDAL: Ummm . . . You know I hadn't thought about
the consequences then and there. Obviously, ah, you
know, um, you know I wasn't thinking about getting
caught. I wasn't thinking about the consequences then
the next day, you know, I realized what I did and we
went from there, but it was too late to do anything.

OSN: **And . . . do you regret ripping up that plant?**

VANDAL: Yes. You know, I tried to do as much good to the
community as possible, you know, that I, you know,
live around, so yeah, I mean . . . yeah.

OSN: **And what do you have to say to all the people who
spent their time and money making it look nice only
for you to trash it?**

VANDAL: Yeah, I have to say I'm sorry obviously. If I was
someone who, you know, who decorated the community and planted plants around the community and

[was] more involved in the community I would not let that happen so . . .

OSN: And do you recall on April 2 there hasn't been any vandalism at the Commons? Why would we believe you haven't been doing this for months?

VANDAL: Well, I believe that one of the other times that you caught someone on camera or whatever who were doing the vandalism I was on spring break, so I wasn't here. So that was one other time I had an alibi to your accusations. But other than that, you really just need to take my word. I have no previous record of vandalism or anything else. For the most part, you just have to take my word that I'm a nice person.

OSN: Are you going to pay a fine?

VANDAL: Well, I'm taking care of that right now at the court we will see with that . . . so . . .

OSN: And . . . is there anything else you want to say to the people of Selinsgrove?

VANDAL: Umm, I'm not a terrible person that, you know, your article indicated sometimes that I'm a menace and a vandal. All I did was pull a plant and I'm sorry that I did that but I'm a good respectful person around the Susquehanna and Selinsgrove community and you know I'm sorry that I did the one thing that I did but yeah . . . that's not who I am . . . and yeah . . .

Did I believe him that he only did it the one time? Not really. But my job as a reporter is to give the facts without commentary. I would honor my agreement with the vandal—he gave me a long, on-the-record interview so I would take down his name—and let my readers decide for themselves if they thought he was being honest.

Since I broke the news of the homicide, being in Selinsgrove was a little like living inside a fishbowl. It seemed wherever I went, all eyes were on me. No one ever approached me saying mean things, but I definitely felt some angry stares. Glenn, the manager of the Kind Cafe, would tell me that people were talking about me in there, saying not very nice things.

Then there were my supporters—people who had been following the *OSN* since the beginning, and people who saw me on the news who thought what I did was cool.

And another thing became clear: the people who had power in the town—local politicians and law enforcement—were the ones who disliked me the most. Meanwhile, the people without power in the town, usually those without a lot of money or a fancy title, had become my biggest supporters. They approached me constantly: on the street, in the grocery store, inside the Kind Cafe. They always had such nice things to say to me, but it was getting a little overwhelming. I decided this would be the perfect time to go stay with Mimi and Pop-Pop for a few days.

Right before I left, I wrote up my story and posted a transcript of the interview with the plant vandal. Because Izzy handled all the online stuff, I asked her to go through and remove the vandal's name, per our deal. Then I left and thought of nothing except watching movies with my Mimi and going through old photos with Pop-Pop.

But while I was away, the vandal began to panic. Apparently it would take a few days for the name to actually disappear from the online versions of my story. So, when he googled his name, the first thing that still came up was my stories. The plant vandal began e-mailing me constantly, but I had made my mind up that I wouldn't check my e-mail while I was away. Finally, the vandal somehow got my mom's phone number and called her.

"I don't think she believed me," he told my mom, somewhat pan-icked. "I'm really sorry. What can I do? I really need to get a job."

My mom calmly explained that I had agreed to take his name down, but that it wouldn't take effect for a few days. When they got off the phone, she called me, laughing like crazy.

"Words have so much power, Hilds," she said after she stopped laughing. "Just keep doing what you're doing, and you'll be able to change anything you want, just by telling the truth."

30

TRUTH TO POWER

AFTER EXPERIENCING MY "FAME," I settled into a new normal. In this new version of my life, I was still a little girl who played with dolls and hung out with her best friend. I was a sister and a daughter and a granddaughter. A homeschooler and a reporter. But things were amplified. Turned up. Because of the attention I received from breaking the news of the homicide, I had many more subscribers and many, many more people sending me news tips. As a result, I began covering more serious stories.

Over the next few years, I investigated corruption in a local fire department that resulted in top officials losing their jobs. My exclusive reporting on an alleged KKK member ended with the person being fired and leaving town. My coverage of a drug problem at the local high school inspired district-wide policy change. More than ever, I understood the power of telling the truth. It's like the Peter Parker principle from Spider-Man: "With great power comes great responsibility." My reporting had to be accurate when the stakes were so high. While I took this duty very seriously, it felt more exhilarating than anxiety producing.

But almost all at once, it seemed like my whole family needed a change of scenery. The gossip about us was like an endless swarm of buzzing bees. It affected Izzy's social life. Even though she wasn't one to act like she cared what people thought of her, it wasn't easy being the older sister of the kid who broke up the drug ring at the school. Kids were nervous around her, fearing that if they did something wrong, it might end up in the news.

My mom and dad had a similar issue. The people who weren't cautious around them seemed to be endlessly fascinated by talking about the gossip—gossiping about the gossip, if you will. This made my parents crazy. They couldn't seem to go anywhere without people telling them nasty things they read on social media about me. Even though my parents announced to everyone that they had a policy of not reading comments, the people they met seemed to think the gossip *they* had was important enough that my parents would want to know.

They were wrong. It got so bad that at a barbecue one day, my dad had to rescue my mom from someone who had practically shoved an iPad in her face after she politely refused to read the comments. It may have been interesting party conversation for the other person, but this was our life, and we wanted no part in the negativity.

So in March 2018, we packed the car and took a road trip. It was my dad's idea. He began looking for an Airbnb that we could stay in for a month. His only criteria were that it was in a warm place and didn't cost too much money. He began looking in Florida, but it was difficult to find a place that would take four kids and two dogs and didn't cost a ton of money. So he kept moving west until he found a little house in a little town in southern Arizona called Patagonia. We knew nothing about it aside from the fact that the weather was forecast to be above seventy degrees with sunshine. Deal.

We took four or five days to drive there. It was so much fun seeing how the landscape changed along the way. We stopped in some interesting spots like Nashville and Albuquerque and ate some

Hilde, eleven, looking decidedly "East
Coast" on the family's first trip to Arizona.

delicious foods. (I'm talking to you, Nashville-style ribs.) Don't get
me wrong—packing four kids and two dogs into one car was chaos.
During one particularly long, boring stretch in Texas, Izzy decided to
play a little game of Truth or Dare with us. She dared Juliet, who was
three at the time, to pick Georgie's nose. As Juliet went to do this, the
car hit a pothole and not only did her finger go into Georgie's nose,
it did it with a great deal of force. Within seconds, Georgie's nose
was gushing blood and both my little sisters were crying hysterically.
My parents, fairly unfazed by this point into their parenting journey,
just pulled over and laughed. Eventually, and with a small degree of
surprise, we all made it in one piece.

Patagonia, Arizona, is a town of nine hundred people eighteen miles north of the Mexican border that developed in the mid-1900s as a trading center for the nearby mines and ranches. It is known as part of the Sky Islands for its high elevation and gigantic mountain ranges. To us, it looked like a movie set for an old western made a baby with your aunt Gertrude who always talks about her time in San Francisco and smells like patchouli. Not that that was a bad thing. We all fell immediately in love.

The vibe was similar to the Island of Misfit Toys from *Rudolph the Red-Nosed Reindeer*. Everyone we met seemed to have come from some crazy place across the world and they all had their own story of how they made their way to Patagonia. Obviously, we fit right in. By the second week of our stay, my parents bought a house and decided we would begin spending each winter in Patagonia.

My dad and I talked a lot about what I would do with the *Orange Street News* during the five months we were away. I had subscribers all around the world at this point. I could stop reporting for those months and offer a refund, but at this stage I couldn't imagine not working on my paper for so long. I decided that I could try to report from Patagonia. If I couldn't get enough news to fill an issue, I decided I could just include longer fiction stories.

But as it turned out, I didn't have to find the news—the news found me. One day, just a few weeks into our stay, I saw the marshal zooming down the street with his lights on. I was already on my bike, so I gave chase. There had been reports of a mountain lion hanging out in someone's backyard, and I thought maybe there had been another sighting. But when the marshal saw me following him, he approached me. He told me that it was illegal for me to be following him.

I wonder if he ever looks back on this moment with regret. What I know for sure is that he should. Remember the lesson I learned in Charleston about citizen journalism? I definitely did. As the marshal's tone turned menacing, I pulled out my cell phone and began recording. In the video, you can hear the marshal tell me it is illegal to put his face on the Internet (it's not—he's a public official, not a private citizen), and he gave me a "lawful order" to stop following him. Then he actually threatened to arrest me!

Here is the story I published, complete with the video, as soon as I got home.

Patagonia Marshal Threatens to Arrest OSN Publisher
SEE THE VIDEO
By Hilde Kate Lysiak
The OSN was working on a story in Patagonia, Arizona when a law enforcement officer threatened the reporter with arrest unless she stopped reporting the news.

The OSN was biking down Roadrunner Lane investigating the tip at about 1:30 pm on February 18th when the reporter was stopped by Patagonia Marshal Joseph Patterson and asked for identification.

The Orange Street News identified herself as a member of the media, including name and phone number.

"I don't want to hear about any of that freedom of the press stuff," said Patterson.

The Marshal continued "I'm going to have you arrested and thrown in juvey."

The Marshal didn't have his lights on and passed several people who were on the streets without stopping them or questioning them.

"I can have you arrested, do you understand?" the Marshal answered.

Asked what she could be arrested for, the officer first said it was for "disobeying his command," then said it was for riding on the wrong side of the road. Finally, the officer said a Mountain Lion was spotted in the area despite there being other people in the area who were not kicked off the road.

"I'm worried about your safety, the area you were in we were dealing with a mountain lion," said Patterson.

"I gave you a lawful order and if you disobey a law enforcement officer. . . . Lying to me and saying you were going to your friend's house wasn't acceptable."

"If you paste my face on the internet it's against the law so I'm not giving you permission to use my picture or my face on the internet, do you understand all that?"

The OSN answered, "I understand all that."

The court says the First Amendment gives citizens the right to record police officers in public while they are performing their duties. But that doesn't mean you're allowed to record if you're doing so secretly interfering with the officer, or otherwise breaking the law.

The Officer told the reporter he was calling her parents.

"You aren't an adult so don't act like it," Marshal Patterson said before driving off.

Within a few hours of posting my story and video, and three years after breaking the news of the homicide, I went viral again. If I had felt like I was in a fishbowl in Selinsgrove, it was like I was a walking aquarium in Patagonia. There were only nine hundred residents, so it felt like literally everyone was staring at me. The day after the video went viral, I was in the market buying a drink when a woman who worked at the local café, also the daughter of the town mayor, approached me.

"You'd better take that down if you know what is good for you," she threatened. "You have no idea what you just did."

Not quite the welcome my family was hoping for.

But the media frenzy was intense. Everyone from fellow journalists to lawyers and judges (even the American Civil Liberties Union!) was posting about how unconstitutional what the marshal did was. One of my favorite quotes that sums up my defense of the First Amendment was from the president of the Society of Professional Journalists (of which I am the youngest member), J. Alex Tarquinio. She said: "She is holding the powerful accountable and demonstrating the qualities of a good, ethical, persistent journalist."

I think I like that quote so much because it speaks to what my intentions were that day that I began filming. Many people misunderstood me, even people who were my biggest fans. They called me precocious, a rabble-rouser, a bada**. Others accused me of just trying to generate popularity. But there was nothing in me that enjoyed my confrontation with the marshal. It made me feel sad and scared. And very angry. The government is supposed to protect the people, and often it does. But just like in any profession, there are some bad people. If the public didn't have the right to hold these people accountable, then our freedom would be in jeopardy. I also knew from working with my dad that the right to tape an officer extended beyond my ability to report the news. In many poor communities, when police officers commit crimes, often no one believes the victim. A video can be their only defense. This is why it is so important to know our rights. If I didn't, a corrupt marshal would still be policing the town of Patagonia. For anyone needing a refresher:

> The First Amendment: Congress shall make no law respecting an establishment of religion, or prohibiting the free exercise thereof; or abridging the freedom of speech, or of the press; or the right of the people peaceably to assemble, and to petition the Government for a redress of grievances.

Unlike after the homicide, this time I decided to refuse all media requests. I wanted my work to speak for itself. But even without my participation, thousands of news stories were generated in nearly every major paper across the country.

Luckily, the media backlash against the marshal seemed to change the minds of many of the people angry with me. The woman from the market stopped me to say she was sorry, and at a town meeting a few nights later, her mother, the mayor, issued a formal apology to me: "The governing body for the town of Patagonia would like to apologize for the First Amendment rights violation inflicted upon Hilde Lysiak, a young reporter in our community. We are sorry, Hilde. We encourage and respect your continued aspiration as a successful reporter."

Another victory for free speech!

Life settled down in the following weeks. People in Patagonia seemed to have better things to do than to worry about what I was up to. It was nice that I felt like I had some breathing room, but I wasn't feeling especially great. There are many changes that happen when you are twelve, and I don't think I was ready for them. But like it or not, the changes were coming. I knew I couldn't stay a little girl forever, but I had no idea how hard the transition was going to be.

31

LOSING PERSPECTIVE

WHEN I BECAME A TEENAGER, truth was no longer simple. Truth was like playing a game of tag with a shadow—constantly out of reach. The more I chased after it, the more it moved away.

In the summer of 2019, my family decided to settle in Patagonia permanently. Just a few months after my run-in with the marshal, we found ourselves, dogs and all, again stuffed into the car driving back to Selinsgrove to handle the sale of our home. What I had told my family (and what I thought was true at the time) was that I really wanted to live in Patagonia year-round. But when we began packing up our house, it no longer felt true. I reasoned with myself: it's normal to feel sad when you leave a place you've lived. But the sadness seemed to follow me wherever I went.

Before going back to Patagonia, we made a family trip to Italy. For a month, we traveled all around the country, seeing sights, eating amazing food, and visiting my dad's relatives. This was something I had wanted to do for so long, but the actual doing of it did not bring the joy I had imagined. I always thought I loved traveling. Was that no longer true? I remember sitting in the kitchen of an apartment we had rented in Lecce. This is one of the most beautiful cities in Italy. It sits way down on the heel of the country between the Ionian and Adriatic Seas and is full of amazing old baroque-style buildings. The apartment had stone walls and a fireplace in the kitchen. I remember sitting on a little couch next to that fireplace with my mom, tears rolling down my cheeks, telling her that even though I didn't know why, I just felt so sad.

"This is a rough time in a girl's life, Hilds. There are so many changes," my mom said for probably the hundredth time in the previous six months.

And she was right. I no longer recognized myself. Not only had my body changed from looking like a little girl's to that of a young woman, but I had gained a lot of weight. During that stay, with the sea so close, my family went to the beach often. If they wouldn't let me hang back in the apartment by myself, I would sit on the sand in shorts and a baggy T-shirt. It wasn't that I didn't love the water—it's just that the self-consciousness I felt over my new body overrode any possible joy I would have had swimming. When I look back on the photographs taken during that trip, I stand apart from my family in nearly each one—the physical distance is a representation of how disconnected and alone I was feeling.

Back in Patagonia, I kept reporting, but the sadness made me so much less motivated than I had been in all the years of the *Orange Street News*. Almost my whole identity was based on being a reporter. Was that all a lie too? Just like after my grandparents died, I sought comfort in food. At this point, my parents felt I was too old for them to be controlling my eating anymore. But without their restrictions, I found myself totally *out* of control.

I began to binge. Binge eating is when a person eats large amounts of food and feels unable to stop. Because I knew my parents—especially my mom—would freak out if they knew, I began to hide it. I would walk to the market and stock up on ice cream and junk food and then store it where they couldn't see it. I would wait to eat until my parents went to sleep, or I would say I was taking a bath and sit in the bathroom filling myself with so much junk that I felt sick. The worst part was the guilt I felt afterward. I knew I was doing something that wasn't good for me, but I couldn't seem to stop. And, of course, it made me keep gaining weight.

During this time, I felt like I went from being someone my parents were proud of to being something that caused them stress. Inevitably, they found all the empty junk food containers hiding around the house and figured out what was going on. They were both very worried about me, but being very different people, they could not agree on how to handle my sadness and disordered eating.

This is how a typical conversation between them would go (I still had a knack for eavesdropping):

"I think we need to get her some help," my mom would say.

"That's crazy—how could a stranger possibly help? We're her parents; no one knows her better than we do," my dad would answer.

"But we *don't* know what we're doing, Matt. If we control her eating, she becomes sadder and more withdrawn. If we don't control her eating, she binges and her mood is all over the place. I have no clue how to handle this."

"She's a thirteen-year-old girl. This is a hard time. She'll pull through," my dad would say.

The one thing they were on the same page about was sending me to school. They began using the words "typical kid experience," as if that was going to be the cure for all my problems. Highest on the list of typical kid experiences they felt I needed was attending the public middle school. They might as well have painted a bright red bull's-eye on my back as they sent me out the door.

First of all, I was one of only seven kids in the entire class. In a town as small as Patagonia, everyone knew one another. Most of the kids in my class had grown up together since they were babies. Some of them were even related. Many of them came from families that did not approve of my coverage of the marshal.

And then, if that wasn't bad enough, another big story broke. There was an old television show that my grandmothers used to watch called *Murder She Wrote*. In it, the main character, a mystery writer named Jessica Fletcher, seemed to find herself in the center of the story. And it's not like she was hanging out in the rough neighborhoods of a big city. This all happened in a formerly quiet little town in coastal Maine. It was like murder followed her around. Great for her book writing, not so great for the town.

See where this is going? I didn't. So when I got a tip that there had been a stabbing in safe and small Patagonia, the surprise made me jump into action. Fortunately, it turned out that no one died. Even though this time there was only an "attempted first-degree murder," the story was just as tragic as the homicide had been in Selinsgrove. A local woman in her thirties was stabbed several times with an ice pick by her former boyfriend. The suspect was on the loose, and to complicate matters, the marshal refused to identify the suspect either by name or picture. I was proud that the *Orange Street News* was able to get this important information to the people.

Despite surviving, the woman was badly injured. Perhaps even worse, her eleven-year-old daughter was witness to the crime and the one to heroically call 911. Guess where she went to school?

The night before the daughter of the stabbing victim was due to return to school, my dad pulled me aside to have a talk. Even though she was a grade below me, in a school as small as ours there was no chance we wouldn't run into each other. I was definitely a little nervous about how she would react to my coverage of her mother's case. Even though I reported only the facts and even withheld her mom's name for several days, I knew from experience that people don't always want the truth getting out.

"Have compassion, but never apologize for reporting truth," was my dad's advice.

The next day, I walked into the bathroom to pee and (of course!) almost ran smack into the girl.

"Why did you report about my mom?" she asked.

She didn't yell at me; she just said it in a sort of sad, matter-of-fact way. My heart was racing. I couldn't imagine all the pain and fear she was feeling. I almost felt like crying.

Instead, I said: "I am so sorry for what your family is going through. I wish that never happened. But unfortunately it did, and I was just doing my job. The suspect was on the loose in town. The people needed to know, and as a reporter, it was my job to tell them. I never wanted to hurt you or your family."

"Whatever," she said, and walked out.

By the time COVID-19 hit a few months later, I was barely speaking to anyone at school. The trailer for *Home Before Dark* had been released, and that only made me feel more like an alien. My parents wanted me to have a typical kid experience, but the bottom line was I just wasn't a typical kid. Not that I even knew *who* I was anymore. I compared the words the media used to describe me—reporter/rebel/hero/prodigy—with the ones kids at school used: nerd/show-off/stuck-up/liar. None of them really felt like they fit.

Trust me when I say I didn't shed one tear when my school closed down because of COVID-19. But as was the case for many kids around the world in the same situation, being stuck at home only made me withdraw more from normal life. When Season 1 of *Home Before Dark* finally came out on April 3, 2020, my family planned a little viewing party. My dad even went out and bought a huge TV for the occasion. But I couldn't imagine sitting in a room with everyone else watching it. I felt anxious around other people—even my own family. So I watched it alone in my bedroom.

It was one of the most surreal moments of my life. Even though the show is not true to my life, the fact that I inspired something so amazing left me speechless. Eventually I lost myself in the intrigue of the show and went on to binge the entire season in a day, but for the entire first episode, my mind was a swirl of confusion.

Who was that girl who inspired the show? Where did she go? Was she ever even real?

32

HELP

THE BREAKING POINT WAS UNEXPECTED. I had been simmering in my sadness for close to two years—a slow boil that felt like it could go on endlessly. On the outside it looked like I had everything. At the age of fourteen, I was the youngest author in the country to publish a book series. My work had inspired a television show, and thousands of news articles told me I was the greatest thing since Taylor Swift's *Red* album. But on the inside, I felt nothing except pain.

The sadness was interrupted temporarily when my parents, in yet another attempt at cheering me up, decided to send me to see Kristen back in Selinsgrove for a month. Prior to this trip, my mom began asking me to take a break from the *OSN*. I had been doing the bare minimum to keep the paper alive, but my heart was certainly not in it. She was the first to see what my dad and I couldn't—that I had, at least for the time being, outgrown it.

"Do you want to stop, Hilds?" my dad would ask. "You don't owe anybody anything. You can stop whenever you feel like it."

"No!" I would shout. The idea of quitting was too terrifying to even consider. But it was my mom who would make me really angry.

"Hilds, this is a time in your life where you are supposed to be a little confused about who you are. It's all part of growing up. Sometimes you need to push the old things away to find out what really fits you now."

I think that deep down I must have known she had a point. I was just nowhere near ready to even consider it. Instead, I fought with her. In the end, I lost the battle and my parents made me take a break. I don't remember exactly how they explained it to me. Something like "Blah blah typical kid blah blah blah . . ."

Right before we left to drive to Selinsgrove, I put a message on the *Orange Street News* website that said: "The Orange Street News is on temporary hiatus as my family has been on the road. Please check back for updates. Thank you!"

My dad and I also seemed unable to get along. My sadness was frustrating for him. He's a fixer. When he has a problem, he makes lists of solutions and sets about trying them one by one until he gets it right. But I don't think he has ever felt as down as I did. The kind of down where you can't even remember that there is an up. You lose touch with all the things that used to make you happy. So I could have written a list, and believe me, I did try, but I still couldn't connect to the joy those things used to bring.

My dad didn't get that. Sometimes he thought I just wasn't trying hard enough. "You need to get out of bed. Take a shower. See a friend," he'd say. "I wouldn't feel happy either if I lay in this dark room all day."

"Sorry to be such a disappointment!" I'd yell back.

Looking back, I think their sending me to Selinsgrove was probably just as much for them as it was for me. And it did end up being exactly what we all needed. It's just that things were going to have to get worse before they could get better. The trip to see Kristen sped that up. I actually had a good time while I was away. I was even able to feel some joy. I didn't have the pressure of my parents' expectations—no one was harassing me about how much I slept, no one was talking to me about my feelings, and no one was checking in with me on my eating. But when it was time for me to leave, the sadness and anxiety reared up again.

In the meantime, the rest of my family was vacationing in Sioux Falls, South Dakota. They had been there for a week before I was to fly out to meet them. As soon as I boarded the plane, I was hit by a terrible sinking feeling. It wasn't that I was just sad leaving Selinsgrove and Kristen. I realized I was dreading being back with my family. I didn't want to fight with them anymore and I didn't want to go back to the same old patterns. But what would be different?

When I got to Sioux Falls, I fell apart in a way I hadn't before. I had a hard time not crying. And I couldn't just sleep it away like I had been trying to. The sadness was like a living, breathing monster inside me that never rested.

Soon after I arrived, a stupid argument with my parents over me not unpacking my suitcase spiraled into me yelling that I did not want to be alive anymore. It wasn't the first time I had thought that—not by a long shot—but it was the first I had said it out loud. Looking back, I know it wasn't that I was actively planning on hurting myself; I just wanted to stop feeling so terrible. The problem was, I couldn't find a way for that to happen.

So on the second or third morning in Sioux Falls, my mom woke me up and said we were going on a walk. There was a beautiful park with sunken gardens just a few blocks from where we were staying. We took a seat among the flowers and sat in complete silence for what felt like a really long time.

Finally, she spoke. Finally, I was ready to hear her.

———————

I began counseling as soon as we were back in Patagonia. After seeing how terrible I was feeling, and especially after I expressed my wish to no longer live, my dad was finally on board with the decision.

Talking with someone who didn't know me helped more than I could ever have imagined. There was something very freeing about not having to worry about disappointing my counselor or hurting her feelings. It took a few sessions for me to relax enough to really open up, but once I did, a bit of the sadness went away. She helped me understand that I was afraid of stopping the paper because I thought it was *the thing* that made me special. Who would I be without it? Just some boring, average person? Who would love me then?

As helpful as counseling was, I wasn't improving as much as everyone expected. My mood was still incredibly low. I was anxious and having trouble sleeping. I had no energy, and my skin was still breaking out. I was working on some techniques to help with my issues with food and eating, but that wasn't much better either.

Finally, my counselor had a meeting with my mom. "There's just a piece of this that doesn't seem to be budging," she said. "I think it might be time we think about medication."

Before my mom would consider putting me on an antidepressant, she insisted I go to get a full medical workup. My counselor suggested a nurse practitioner who is known for getting to the root cause of issues like depression and anxiety. Twenty tubes of blood later, the results were in: I had several underlying health conditions, including vitamin B deficiency and iron deficiency anemia, that were contributing to my depression. I also had some blood sugar and insulin disturbances related to my years of disordered eating. While I didn't need antidepressants, I did need vitamin therapy and dietary change. I still continue to work on my eating patterns with my counselor. But all in all, it seems a small price to pay to feel better.

And I am feeling better. Within the first week of taking the vitamins, I felt my energy begin to return. Soon the sadness and anxiety began to lift. It wasn't like I just woke up one morning feeling fantastic—it was much more subtle than that. I started to notice little things like wanting to be around my family more. At dinner, when

Izzy started to debate ideas with my parents, instead of running off to my room, I found myself joining in the lively discussions. I started going on long walks and began preferring to be outside instead of home lying in my bed.

But the biggest change was that I started to have hope. Hope that I might lead a happy life after all. It feels like I was looking at life through dirty glasses, and starting treatment has wiped them clean.

Just because my perspective is clearer now that the sadness is gone doesn't mean I am happy all the time. I am still a fourteen-year-old girl trying to figure out exactly who I am. Six months ago, I couldn't be bothered to change out of the same black hoodie. Now, there are piles of clothes all over my floor. It's not totally unlike playing dress-up as a little kid, except instead of trying to be a ballerina or a princess, I'm just trying to be me. Whoever she is.

Once schools reopened (at least part-time here in Arizona), I transferred to a large high school twenty minutes away from Patagonia. Considering my less-than-stellar track record with public schooling, I was reluctant, to say the least. But without the constant anxiety I had been feeling, it wasn't that big of a deal for me to give it a try. Now I've gone from never wanting to leave the darkness of my bedroom to actually looking forward to meeting new people.

As I write this, it's only been a few weeks, so it's not like my calendar is jam-packed, but I definitely have some promising leads on friendships. So far, no one has mentioned anything related to my paper. It's not that I'm hiding it from them. It's just that I want people to get to know me for who I am and not only the things I have done.

After years of covering other people's stories, I feel like my own is just beginning. It's still untitled and the words are yet to be written.

But I've never been one to shy away from a story.

AFTERWORD

———

THE SUN IS BLAZING as I begin the long hike up the driveway to our house. I tilt my chin upward and let it hit me full in the face. The brightness outside me, lighting up every rock and newly sprouting seed, mirrors how I am feeling inside.

Moments ago, I sat next to my parents down at the little guesthouse my dad uses as his office, Skyping with the writers and producers of *Home Before Dark*. Season 2 has wrapped, and they have booked the writers' room for the third season (hopefully to be picked up). Even though the story line of the show is made up, the writers have always done a great job at trying to keep the characters' personalities and relationships true to our family. Today they wanted to check in to see what was new before they began writing the next season.

After taking a deep breath and with an army of butterflies in my stomach, I spoke: "I'm no longer doing the paper."

I braced myself for the moment when everything would come crashing down. I waited for the looks of panic and disappointment on their faces. After all, how can you write a show based on a reporter when the reporter is no longer reporting? I could see the headlines now: KID PRODIGY IS A QUITTER! TEEN REPORTER JUST AN AVERAGE GIRL! REAL-LIFE TELEVISION SHOW INSPIRATION A FRAUD! I imagined millions of dollar bills catching fire in the air one by one. In my mind, I saw the television set being torn down—a sort of stop-motion reverse of all the promise new beginnings hold.

But the panic and disappointment never came. When I looked into the face of Dana Fox, the lead writer for the show, what I saw instead was openness and curiosity. So I kept going. I told the writers and producers everything, from the sadness to my issues with food, my decision to put the *Orange Street News* on hold indefinitely, and even the fact that I was realizing I like girls as much as I like boys.

An hour later, nearly everyone on the Skype call had tears rolling down their faces. Many of the writers shared their own stories about how difficult their adolescence was. Some of them had even dealt with depression. The support was overwhelming.

"*You* are incredible, Hilde. The paper was just a cool thing you did. We love and support you no matter what," said Dana.

When I began writing this book, I knew the moment would come when I would have to break the news to my readers that I am no longer reporting. The urge has been strong to wrap this story up with a tidy little bow, to give answers to all the lingering questions: *What will she do now? Is she ever going to report again?* I've fought hard against that urge, because the truth is, I don't know. As with all my stories, I presented the facts as best I could; I told the truth. Yet I am aware of the matter of perspective.

Some of you may feel cheated. If this were a Choose Your Own Adventure book, this would not be the outcome you'd have picked. To you I say, I get it. When I began my story, it wouldn't have been my choice either. You wanted a hero. Maybe I wanted to be a hero.

But I changed. I *grew*. I wish for you the acceptance of a million messy changes, because trust me, like it or not, they will come.

Some of you may feel understood. If this were a Choose Your Own Adventure book, you'd also pick a different ending, but you know that life doesn't work that way. You may have gone through similar struggles as I have. You weren't looking for a hero. You wanted a living, breathing human, complete with flaws, to offer some hope. To you I say, here I am.

In retelling this story, I feel I am beginning to gain a bit of my own perspective. I am neither a "complete joke" nor "heroic." I am neither "ignorant" nor a "prodigy." My work was not "sensationalist trash," nor was it that of the "future savior of journalism."

I am just Hilde. And I'm starting to know and like who that person is a little more every day.

Hilde, fourteen, hanging out on vacation in San Antonio.

ACKNOWLEDGMENTS

If you change the way you look at things, the things you look at change.
—Dr. Wayne Dyer

THIS BOOK WOULD never have been possible without the unconditional love and support of so many people who stuck by me throughout all my changes, good and bad.

The first person I'd like to thank is my mom, Bridget Lysiak, who for months woke up at 4:00 AM to help make this book a reality. I should probably mention that she also worked as a teacher and a nurse all while raising me and my three sisters. And we are a lot. Thanks, Mom. I love you.

My dad, Matthew Lysiak, for having the guts to take a four-year-old to cover a shooting in a housing project. Both your work and your parenting have been among the biggest inspirations of my life.

My sisters—Izzy, Georgie, and Juju, I'm so thankful I'll always have you to understand just how crazy our parents are.

Hilde, thirteen, with CNN's Christiane Amanpour
as they accept awards for press freedom.

My grandmother, Candace Thrash. You've always been a rock,
especially during my darkest days. And where would I be without our
coffee rides to Nogales? I hope you know how much I appreciate you.

My Mammy and Pop-Pop, whose ability to tell stories and keep
the past alive inspired me greatly.

My best friend, Kristen Freed, who has been there from Barbies
to breakdowns. Thank you.

Other people who have contributed to making this book a real
thing include the great people at Chicago Review Press, especially Jerry
Pohlen, who took a chance on a memoir of a fourteen-year-old kid
with more issues than a newspaper. Thanks, too, to CRP managing
editor Devon Freeny, cover designer Natalya Balnova, and copyeditor
Elizabeth Yellen. Thank you to my manager, Sharlene Martin, whose
unrivaled work ethic allowed this book to hit the shelves. You have

been a good friend to the family. Thank you, Sharlene. Brooklynn Prince, you inspire me with your spirit. Don't ever let anyone dim that light. Joy Gorman Wettels and Dana Fox, thank you for demonstrating to me how possible it is to be powerful *and* kind.

There are also two people I think about every day who need to be mentioned: my grandparents, Gina and Arthur Lysiak, who were my biggest fans and first subscribers. I miss you terribly but am so appreciative of the short time we had together.